BUILDING A STRATEGIC CHURCH

'You can't build a healthy church without an intentional strategy. David Beer eloquently focuses on the concepts and tools that pastors need to lead their church to be all that God is asking of us.'

RICK WARREN

GW00319965

To my grandchildren
Brianna, Jackson and Jonah

Building
a Strategic
Church

DAVID BEER

KINGSWAY PUBLICATIONS
EASTBOURNE

Unless otherwise indicated, Bible quotations are from
the New International Version and Inclusive Language edition
© 1973, 1978, 1984 by the International Bible Society.
NLT = New Living Translation
© 1996 by Tyndale Charitable Trust.
AV = Authorised Version (Crown copyright).
TLB = The Living Bible © Tyndale House Publishers 1971.

Design for the cover by CCD (www.ccdgroup.co.uk)

Typeset by Alliance Interactive Technology.

ISBN 978–1–84291–288–1

KINGSWAY COMMUNICATIONS LTD
Lottbridge Drove, Eastbourne BN23 6NT, England.
Email: books@kingsway.co.uk

Printed in the USA

Contents

Acknowledgements

This page is one of the last to be compiled, but the book could not have been written without the help and support of the people mentioned below.

The four churches I have served throughout my ministry gave me the experiences from which I write this book. To the congregations of Meredith Road Baptist Church, Coventry, Emmanuel Baptist Church, Gravesend, Tonbridge Baptist Church and Frinton Free Church, I want to say a big thank you. Thank you for your patience, grace and encouragement through all the years of pastoral ministry and church leadership.

My particular thanks go to Lewis Drummond with whom I served as an associate pastor in Louisville, Kentucky, and who is now part of that 'great cloud of witnesses' mentioned in Hebrews 12:1; Rick Warren, Pastor of Saddleback Church, California, and author of *The Purpose Driven Church* and *The Purpose Driven Life*; and Hubert Janisch, also part of that 'great cloud of witnesses' and the pastor from whom I heard the call of God to ministry many years ago.

I would also like to thank Richard Herkes, Publishing Director of Kingsway Publications, and Carolyn Owen, Editorial Co-ordinator, for their huge encouragement and support. A big thank you is also due to Ann Rudland, my Personal Assistant, who typed most of the pages of this book and contributed helpful insights along the way.

My wife, Dorothy, has been a great support, along with my children and grandchildren: Leisa married to a pastor, Steve, and the proud parents of Brianna and Jack; Keith married to Faith and the proud parents of Jonah.

I never dreamed I would write a book, but this is my fourth. Most of all I want to say thank you to God for giving me the privilege of this opportunity to encourage church members and leaders through sharing my experiences of following the call of God in ministry. To him is all the glory.

Foreword

The young man is sitting around the table with business associates in a fine restaurant. As he takes a bite of food, he begins to choke. As he starts to turn blue and grabs his throat, several people around the table engage in an impassionate discussion of the Heimlich procedure of abdominal thrust and how it works. Meanwhile, the man's situation becomes more desperate by the moment. In a flash, a diner from a nearby table steps in, performs the maneuver, the obstruction flies out of the choking man's mouth, and he is saved. A person at the table says, 'That's just what I was saying.' A voiceover from this television advert says, 'Less Talk,' as the words 'Make It Happen' flash on the screen.

All too often in the realm of Christian leadership, supposed experts theorize with 'much talk' about elaborate strategies for church health/growth, but never 'make it happen' in the trenches of Christian service. David Beer is a writer who has consistently demonstrated the value of strategic leadership throughout his 40 years of ministry. In each of the four churches he served as senior pastor, David led the way in implementing evangelism and discipleship that was blessed by sustained growth in each successive ministry. This growth was noteworthy, considering that the majority of churches in Great Britain continued in a pattern of overall decline.

Thus, his writing in this area is not theoretical, but the practical counsel produced from decades of significant pastoral ministry in the local church. The result is a treasure trove of insight composing the content of his most recent book, *Building a Strategic Church*.

I had the opportunity to serve as David's first full-time associate in ministry for three years in his Tonbridge pastorate, and there experienced first-hand the real value of *team spirit* that led to unified ministry in the church. Key to that leadership was his willingness to share much of the ministry with me – I was given opportunities to preach, marry, take funerals, lead in worship, teach various age groups, pursue creative ministries (with freedom to fail) – and was given affirming counsel along the way. I was careful to submit to his team leadership, and always sought to be loyal to his role as Senior Pastor. At each turn, David was not threatened by any success I had—rather he relished in it, and subsequently that type of leadership with *team spirit* became my model for life.

I witnessed first-hand a pastor who employed strategy in a way that was consistent with biblical patterns. David demonstrated consummate people skills as he developed *relational structures* that promoted organic health/growth in the body of Christ. He consistently proclaimed biblical truth in his sermons, but beyond that, it was *application preaching* that challenged hearers to take personal action in their lives. Working with church leadership, David was committed to *training and equipping* them with practical skills for their ministries. David's exponential thinking in terms of his vision for the future of the church often inspired me, and his abounding trust in God for something greater than might be earthly imagined. David displayed a *generous attitude* towards people, and was a purveyor of God's grace to those who were experiencing struggles in life. David led the church to *involvement with the local community*, cooperating in evangelistic ventures and ecumenical outreach. Most of all, David was a pastor with a *caring heart*, who was willing to spend countless hours as the nurturing under-shepherd of his flock. And he never lost his sense of humour.

Now David Beer is extending his ministry as the Regional Leader of Purpose Driven Church Europe. He is engaging this opportunity in an aggressive manner because he believes in the biblical health/growth principles of this proven process in churches around the world. Through his teaching and direction, he is training leaders to implement strategy that will have a direct impact on the growth of churches all across Europe and beyond.

I believe that this book will serve as a compass for pastors and leaders who are serious about implementing strategy in their particular sphere of Christian leadership. There are useful insights of eternal value here for anyone seeking to learn and grow in their service to God's kingdom. Take to heart the truths contained within, commit to take personal action, and trust God to 'make it happen' in your corner of his vineyard.

Dr Larry Michael
Senior Pastor, First Baptist Church of Sweetwater
Longwood, Florida
(Author of *Spurgeon on Leadership*, Kregel Publications, 2003)

1
Why Be Strategic?

Imagine a church where bruised, addicted, lonely, depressed and anxious people find hope, a purpose for their lives and start to reach out to others.

Imagine a church where people regularly come to faith in Christ and begin to grow as disciples.

Imagine a church where new believers learn how to grow spiritually and begin to live by biblical principles and values.

Imagine a church where people find worship so inspiring and relevant they can't wait to come back.

Imagine a church where people can't wait to get involved in the ministries of the church and to share their new-found faith with work friends, family and social contacts.

Too hard to imagine? For some, it seems that way.

Jim is 40 years old and leads a suburban church of over 250 members. He is an excellent preacher and well respected by the local community. But Jim doesn't feel effective as a leader:

> I can't understand why our church isn't making any real difference to the community as a whole. Violence and vandalism are on the increase. What are we not doing? We've been the same size for over ten years. We don't seem to be seeing many new faces. There are plenty of unchurched people around here, but we're not reaching them.

Ruth is 36 years old and leading a small rural church: 'We don't seem to be making any impact in our village. It doesn't seem to matter what we do. I'm depressed and ready to resign.'

Bill has just received his MA and is leading a church of 300 members, but he is frustrated by a lack of direction:

> I'm not sure I can apply all I've learned. We've got a lot of good things going on in the church, but we're too traditional. Our people seem so satisfied. They don't seem to care about newcomers. They want to keep the church as one big closed family. I don't know if they understand what church is about. I'm not sure I want to perpetuate this way of doing things. How can I get them to think differently?

Doug is an active deacon in a lively church. 'But it doesn't seem to be going anywhere,' he says. 'We have so many meetings and activities, it's wearing me out. It's one meeting after another, sometimes five nights a week. I'm wondering if all the activity and discussion is worth while.'

Steve is pastor of a church of nearly 500 members. He's been there four years:

> The church has been around 500 members for the past fifteen years. I don't know if I can ever take it forward. Somehow it seems stuck. We see all the possibilities for new growth but can't seem to reach new people. Nearly all our new people are transfer growth – people coming from other churches. We've been on a plateau for so long. Maybe I'm the wrong person to lead this church.

These are the kinds of frustration that have been expressed to me over recent years. Christians long to see their churches making a difference in the communities that they serve, and in the larger world, but somehow there is a stalemate that blocks progress. Put simply, there is no strategy for future development.

Where are we going?

Strategic churches are churches that are making a constructive
and positive difference to the lives of people in their community.
But it's not an easy task. What is the future of the church? After
40 years in full-time church leadership I have come to the conclusion, in spite of all the books I have read and conferences I have
attended on the subject, that no one knows. This is for two reasons:

1. Our culture is continually changing.
2. Who knows what God is going to do?

We do not yet know, in what has been referred to as 'post-
Christendom', what shape or form the church will take in the
future. However, there are a few things we do know. We do know
that God will build his church, and we do know that there are
important biblical values and principles that do not change. Yes,
they need to find new expressions, but the principles remain the
same in every generation. It is these principles that form the substance of this book.

This essential strategy for the church comes from the New Testament. There is nothing vague about it. Responding to the mission set for us by Jesus Christ – to make disciples for him – the
church plays its part in God's strategy for growth: 'I planted the
seed, Apollos watered it, but God made it grow' (1 Corinthians
3:6). Thus our overall aim is to let God build his church while we
make disciples.

Beyond the essential biblical strategy for the church, every
church is different according to the make-up of its local community, its distinctive local culture and its age. Is it a newly planted
church or an established one? There are other key factors that
may affect how the essential strategy is developed, such as its style
of worship, the average age of the congregation and its gover-
nance (often set by the denomination or grouping to which it

belongs). The local strategy is worked out when we listen to God, when we look at the community where God has put us and when we work together as a team.

There is, however, one other major factor not always taken into consideration, and it's this: *a strategic church recognises that we are moving into an entirely new era where the church can no longer see itself as an established institution, but as the dynamic movement it was in the first place.*

In stark contrast, some churches unknowingly operate by a default strategy. They do almost everything the way they've always done it. Researchers identify irrelevance as one of the major reasons in the UK for the massive decline in church attendance and the subsequent weakened influence of the church in the local community.

It's all very well to spell out high-sounding aims for the church in rousing tones at Christian conferences, but these are rarely matched by practical strategies and structures designed to reach those aims. It is no longer a matter of convincing Christians to be involved in their community and the world. The majority are already there, in the work place and the neighbourhood. The question now is: how do we equip them to be effective and influential disciples? This is the challenge facing the church today. We have not yet found the structures and strategies that will both create and sustain the disciples of the twenty-first century. 'Setting a goal is not the main thing. It is deciding how you will go about achieving it and staying with that plan.' This is what many churches find difficulty in doing. The quotation is from Tom Landry – well-known coach for the Dallas Cowboys football team. He is talking about strategy.

How do we get there?

This book is not for those who expect to read yet another book on church health and put it on the shelf with all the others. This book is about commitment and intentionality. That is why I've written so much about action and application. It's about 100 per cent commitment to Christ and his church. Ninety-five per cent commitment is like running ninety-five per cent of a marathon . . . it's the last 5 per cent that makes the difference! In this book I shall lay out the principles that apply everywhere. I shall sometimes share examples of my own experiences and struggles as a Christian leader trying to live out the principles I describe, but it will be for you and your colleagues to apply the principles in concrete ways in your locality. As a result, you will find this book heavier on principles and lighter on examples than my previous ones.

Building a Strategic Church is ultimately about helping people everywhere to live strategic lives – lives that count, lives lived by values, principles and purposes that are eternal. We know there is widespread disillusionment with religion, but there is a deep hunger for meaning and purpose, either consciously or unconsciously. It is this hunger that the twenty-first-century Christian church needs to address.

Seeing people grow

Human beings are not designed to be bored. Creativity, purpose and a sense of fulfilment are all natural human inclinations. For various reasons, that realisation can lay buried inside a person for years. Perhaps the family or community environment in which they live has not allowed or stimulated the search for meaning and purpose. It is never acknowledged, and consequently people do not know why they think or behave as they do. That makes people vulnerable to others and capable of being manipulated into unhealthy or destructive purposes. People totally without hope do hopeless things, and people totally without purpose do purposeless things, such as pointless vandalism and random violence.

In complete contrast, those who genuinely discover accurate self-awareness can radically change from compliance or anger to greater understanding of others and a life characterised by constructive purposes. For example, two UK city gang leaders, both racist and violent, one Asian and the other white, had a bitter hatred towards each other until they were sent on a course where they had to share the same room. As they began to understand each other's background and culture, they discovered they liked each other! They now help other teenagers to understand themselves and their emotions.

The Christian community is where a strategy for living life with healthy purposes and hope should be paramount. This requires that such a community is relationally healthy and will help to develop character and the honing of personal skills and talent without manipulation. This in turn requires that the Christian community – the church – builds on the essential strategy to make disciples of Jesus Christ. It may surprise you that one of the most strategic persons ever to walk this planet was Jesus Christ. This is the One who said, 'I will build my church' (Matthew 16:18). Every generation, therefore, needs to ask him what he is building, and how they can get in on it.

What follows in this book is a reminder of tried and tested biblical principles, foundational values that characterise a healthy church. As Rick Warren reminds us, 'There is no single key to church health and church growth; there are many keys. The church is not called to do one thing; it is called to do many things.'[1]

Strategy is inevitable

What do I do now? Where do I go from here? What comes next? These kinds of question are common to everyone at some stage in

---

[1] Rick Warren, *The Purpose Driven Church*, Zondervan 1995, p. 128.

life. They often indicate that we are searching for a strategy to help us cope or move our lives forward. Few of us in the Western world can live without some kind of strategy, though some of us, even some senior church leaders, prefer not to be strategic. Even if we don't deliberately choose to be strategic, strategy is sometimes forced upon us. If you are deep in debt, a strategy to recover from debt may be forced upon you.

Some people choose to be strategic in specific areas of life. They may be very strategic in the area of physical fitness but may be not at all strategic in the area of overall personal development. Perhaps they have never even thought about being strategic in any other area of life. Life just happens. They go with the flow.

People are strategic about all kinds of things, like their career, home improvement, parenting, education, or even a personal ambition such as sailing around the world. Whole football teams have carefully devised strategies without which they would not win many games. Sometimes people have short-term strategies without too much thought, such as planning a simple journey. If we want to arrive at a certain time, we work out what time we shall have to leave, what the method of transportation will be and the route we shall take. In all these ways strategy is a part of life.

A well-known top model and TV presenter said, after reaching celebrity status early on in life, 'What do you do when you've gorged yourself on life and it still doesn't make you happy? What else is there?' In total contrast, the wife of one of the passengers in the doomed United Airlines Flight 93 that crashed to the ground in Somerset County, Pennsylvania on 11th September 2001 said, 'Tom's whole life was about strategy. It was setting a goal and getting to that goal. It was formulating a plan and reaching the outcome that he wanted.' He lived a very strategic life.

The great Victorian preacher Charles Haddon Spurgeon was a strategic leader. He is described by one writer as 'self-controlled, observant, and wise, and he had a homely shrewdness'.[2] He was strategic.

The Bible tells us to be strategic

The New Testament is full of encouragements for us to live strategically for noble purposes.

> For this very reason, make every effort to add to your faith goodness; and to goodness, knowledge; and to knowledge, self-control; and to self-control, perseverance; and to perseverance, godliness; and to godliness, mutual affection; and to mutual affection, love. (2 Peter 1:5–7 NIV Incl.)

That's a strategy for personal growth!

To be strategic with your life is also an expression of gratitude. Many of us have so much compared with others. Taking life for granted is the cause of a lot of unhappiness and resentment.

Some Christians are nervous about using the word 'strategy' in association with the church. 'Strategy' is considered either a military term or modern business jargon. However, God himself is strategic and acts in a purposeful and strategic manner.

God is strategic. The title on the cross of Christ is an involuntary testimony to the strategy of God. The title was written in Greek, Latin and Hebrew, the three great languages of learning, government and religion. Jerusalem was the crossroads of these three cultures, which provided the means by which the gospel spread. No other time in the history of the human race was so definitive.

Greece provided the language for the writing of the New Testament. The church had the benefit of the clarity of Greek thought, and the Greek skill and sharpness in the use of words to

---

[2] Sir W. Robertson Nicoll (ed.), *Introduction to Sermons by Revd C. H. Spurgeon*, Thomas Nelson & Sons 1900, p. 9.

provide a vocabulary that could articulate Christian doctrine. Rome provided the roads and highways for a system of communication and travel that was previously impossible. And so the first strongholds of the Christian church were in places where Roman government and Greek culture had combined the most. Then the Jewish nation provided the religious framework in which to build an awareness of a God of loving purpose and the idea of an *ecclesia*. As one historian has noted,

> Christianity had its roots in Judaism; it appealed to the lofty aspirations of human desire and pathetic depths of human need, as the Greek mind had realised them; and it found the machinery and ideals of the Roman Empire in harmony with its own methods, an instrument fitted to its purpose.[3]

A strategic God invites us to live strategic lives. When he told the parable of the shrewd manager, Jesus said, 'The master commended the dishonest manager because he had acted shrewdly. For the people of this world are more shrewd in dealing with their own kind than are the people of the light' (Luke 16:8).

In Matthew 10:16 Jesus says to his disciples, 'I am sending you out like sheep among wolves. Therefore be as shrewd as snakes and as innocent as doves.' Jesus wants us to be men and women of integrity and clear motives, but he expects us to be 'shrewd'. Jesus is saying that he wants us to be strategic.

Luke 14:28–33 says:

> Suppose one of you wants to build a tower. Will he not first sit down and estimate the cost to see if he has enough money to complete it? For if he lays the foundation and is not able to finish it, everyone who sees it will ridicule him, saying, 'This fellow began to build and was not able to finish.' Or suppose a king is about to go to war against another king. Will he not first sit down and consider whether he is able with ten thousand men to oppose the one coming against him

---

[3] A. R. Whitham, *The History of the Christian Church*, Rivingtons 1954, p. 11.

with twenty thousand? If he is not able, he will send a delegation while the other is still a long way off and will ask for terms of peace. In the same way, any of you who does not give up everything he has cannot be my disciple.

Ephesians 5:15 sums it up well: 'Be very careful, then, how you live – not as unwise but as wise, making the most of every opportunity.'

The value of a life well lived

Geddes MacGregor, a theologian, tells the story of an event that happened when he was just six years of age. He went with his mother to visit his grandmother. While the two women were talking, his grandmother said to his mother, 'I'm so glad you decided to have little Geddes. He's been such a joy to all of us.' The grandmother had no idea that Geddes had overheard what she said. The boy came into the room where the two women were talking and asked his grandmother, 'What do you mean, "I am so glad you decided to have little Geddes?"'

He then learned something that he had never known before. His mother was 48 when she became pregnant. She knew about the dangers of pregnancy for a woman of that age. There had been all kinds of discussion with the doctors and the family about what they should do. She finally, and at a late stage in the pregnancy, decided to go ahead and risk what might happen. This, of course, was what the grandmother was referring to.

This was news to the little six-year-old. He had no idea that all this discussion had taken place prior to his being born. He said a picture came into his mind:

> I was in a line moving step by step up to this great portal, over which was simply written the word 'birth'. And as I made my way, suddenly a hand reached, pulled me from the line, and said, 'You have been disqualified; you can't be born.'

And for the first time in his life it dawned on him that he might never have been, that there was nothing necessary or self-caused about his existence. It was a horrible revelation. But then the picture returned.

Again, he was in a line moving step by step up to the door. Only this time, he was allowed to go through. Geddes MacGregor said that from that moment forward he never took his life for granted. For him, realising how close he came to not being added an incredible vitality to the wonder of being alive.[4]

By contrast, for many people life just happens. They go with the flow. They don't think too much about the direction their life is taking. They live as though they automatically have a long lease on life and there is no need to worry about the future. Sadly, it is only when tragedy strikes that some people are still enough to think on what life is all about.

Unless we are strategic with our lives we are in danger of wasting opportunities. But being strategic requires effort and discipline, which some people are not prepared to give. They are tempted to look for shortcuts to happiness by using drugs, alcohol and sex. There is a price to pay there, even if it does come later.

Ashley Smith in her book *Unlikely Angel*, the story of her kidnap by a killer who subsequently released her, tells her own account of drug-taking. She used to use a drug nicknamed 'ice'. She said,

> I would feel the lift in seconds. Suddenly I was alert and exploding with energy, ready to start getting things done. The first time I ever tried the drug I was like, 'Wow! This is great! I've been depressed . . . and now I feel alive again – like I'm really somebody.' Then the paranoia would set in. I was so strung out, paranoid, and miserable, but I thought I would rather die than quit doing that drug – and I almost did.'[5]

---

[4] From a sermon preached by the Revd Dr John Claypool, Rector of St Luke's Episcopal Church, Birmingham, Alabama, © John Claypool, 1999.

[5] Ashley Smith, *Unlikely Angel*, Zondervan 2005, pp. 66–67.

Who was it that said, 'Good things are paid for in advance. Bad things are paid for afterwards'? Finding your purpose in life and developing a strategy to live it out is all-important. It provides motivation. It helps with decision-making. It saves frustration and stress. It helps build relationships.

Purpose and strategy are worked out in quiet moments, in reflecting with others who are on the same quest, and most of all, by learning from our strategic God. We don't have to make this journey of discovery on our own. We make it in company with others, which is what the authentic Christian church is all about.

The role of the church

Sadly, the church has not always facilitated this. When the church started there was a sense of community in which people flourished, felt significant, cared for each other, served the wider community and were committed to each other as well as to God. That's how it got started, but as we well know, it hasn't always continued that way.

At times, church has been a place of abuse and deep hurt. Even by the second half of the first century, Paul is writing to the Christians in Philippi and saying,

> If you have any encouragement from being united with Christ, if any comfort from his love, if any fellowship with the Spirit, if any tenderness and compassion, then make my joy complete by being like-minded, having the same love, being one in spirit and purpose. (Philippians 2:1–2)

According to the dictionary, being strategic means 'having a carefully devised plan of action to achieve a goal'. Clearly, then, the Christian church has an obligation to be strategic. How else can it fulfil the instructions of Jesus to 'go and make disciples of all nations, baptising them in the name of the Father and of the Son and of the Holy Spirit, and teaching them to obey everything I have commanded you' (Matthew 28:19–20)? When the first disciples heard those words they must have thought, 'How are we going to do this? This is an impossible task.' They must have felt overwhelmed.

But then, soon afterwards, Jesus provided the strategy. 'You will receive power when the Holy Spirit comes on you; and you will be my witnesses in Jerusalem, and in all Judea and Samaria, and to the ends of the earth' (Acts 1:8). They were to start where they were, in Jerusalem, and then move out to the district of Judea, then further out to people of another culture, in Samaria, and then to the ends of the earth. That was the strategy, in headline terms.

One way of thinking through what a local Christian community should be and do is to imagine what would happen if Christ returned in a physical human body and set up his headquarters in the location of that community. If every local church intentionally tried to be Christ to the local community, what a difference it would make to the whole nation!

As Joel Edwards of the UK Evangelical Alliance said,

> Imagine a Church that refuses to settle for the way things are. What might it be like to belong to a Church whose primary preoccupation was not fulfilling internal agendas but meeting its mission to make Jesus known and loved in a real world? A Church concerned not just about getting more people inside the building, but turning out contemporary disciples – disciples equipped to love and serve the world, and see other people come to faith in Christ? A Church called to do more than survive, but energised to escape the gravitational pull of secondary matters that keep us from our primary purpose.[6]

The earthly life of Jesus is summarised by his disciple, Peter, in the New Testament book of Acts. 'You know . . . how God anointed

---

[6] Joel Edwards, *IDEA*, Evangelical Alliance, March/April 2003, p. 3.

Jesus of Nazareth with the Holy Spirit and power, and how he went around doing good and healing all who were under the power of the devil, because God was with him' (Acts 10:38). 'He went around doing good' is how the earthly life of Jesus is summed up. His followers are to do the same, and indeed many have tried to do so across the centuries. The work of Christ continues today and is seen in the lives of many. However, without detracting in any way from the broad work of the church, we have to say that its primary task is to fulfil the Great Commission, to be obedient to the command of Christ to 'go and make disciples'. If we are not doing this, or if this is not happening, we had better ask the question, 'Why not?' Have we given in to the pluralism and consumerism that surround us?

Or have we lost a sense of urgency? If we respond to the message of Christ as he lived it and stated it, and if this is not the only life we live, and if this life does have an effect on the one that follows, then it is sheer selfishness to keep this vital information to ourselves. But quite apart from eternal consequences, how uncaring is it to see people struggling to get a grasp on life and make sense of life, only to withhold from them a message of purpose and hope that can help them? That is about as insane as withholding from the world a cure for cancer. The thought is unbearable.

I hope you can see by now why I believe that the biggest factor in the church's failure to make disciples is lack of strategy. There are, of course, some churches that are strategic, as we shall see later. But there are not enough. In some instances it is because there is a suspicion of this thing called 'strategy'. Mention words such as 'purpose' or 'strategy' or 'infrastructure' in these churches and they will be met with extreme caution, even hostility. Such thinking is considered too worldly. To modernise a church building and make it more attractive and visitor-friendly, not to have a church building at all, to have an intentional plan of church health and growth, or to use modern technology to aid worship are all considered out of order. Even to think in ways of making the Christian message more attractive and easier to understand is considered suspect among some Christians. But as we saw earlier, Jesus commented that 'the people of this world are more shrewd . . . than are the people of the light' (Luke 16:8).

The plight of the poor and needy

The famous country music singer Johnny Cash was known for being dressed in black. In his song 'Man in Black' he says why:

> I wear the black for the poor and beaten down,
> Living in the hopeless, hungry side of town. . .
> I wear the black for those who've never read
> Or listened to the words that Jesus said
> About the road to happiness through love and charity.

The church's greatest resource is the people we already have. We must find ways (strategies) to help them go to those who don't know Christ – with generosity, humility and purpose. There are millions who have never read or listened to the words that Jesus said, and the church needs a strategy to make that happen.

Lack of strategy often results in bad stewardship. Finance, energy and creativity are all wasted. Existing disciples are not being equipped to be disciples in today's culture. They are not being equipped to think Christianly about what they do between 9 and 5, or, for that matter, between 5 and 9.

Ever since the day of Pentecost, the church has broadly followed the strategy of Acts 1:8, but we need to recapture that original vision and essential strategy to obey the Great Commission in our day and our generation. We need to translate and interpret this essential biblical strategy into our twenty-first-century world. We need to work out this strategy to meet the emotional and spiritual needs of the people we rub shoulders with.

How aware are we of basic human needs, particularly in their most acute forms among the most disadvantaged and marginalised, and how much have we done concretely to alleviate such needs?

Jesus had a strategy for meeting people's needs. Notice how he talked in different ways to the various individuals he met. For example, compare his conversations with the woman he met at the well (John 4:7–30) with Zacchaeus (Luke 19:1–10) and Nicodemus (John 3:1–21). Jesus was fully aware that he needed to be strategic in his approach to people. 'For I did not speak of my own accord, but the Father who sent me commanded me what to say and how to say it' (John 12:49).

In an effort to reach their communities, a lot of churches tend to focus on programmes rather than a strategy. Programmes are easier to work with, as materials and resources are often ready-made. They are imported from outside, often from para-church organisations. They have their place, of course, and can prove effective in moving a church forward, but some churches jump from one programme to another, looking for the next one when the present one ends, without any real thought of where they are going and what long-term impact they are having.

Short-term leadership doesn't help here. Members of congregations know that clergy come and clergy go, each with their ideas and visions, whereas church members remain. The congregation gets used to different ideas and changing visions without anything significant actually happening. The result is discouragement on the part of congregation and clergy to engage in a long-term strategy.

The church as sign of the kingdom

We know that the New Testament describes the church as a body, but it also sees it as a fellowship and a family. This means it is not to be treated as a club or organisation. As a fellowship it is intended to be a model of how people who inevitably are different from one other can live and work together.

Paradoxically, the church as a sign of hope through its example and service to others is also the world's enemy, often persecuted and despised, because it challenges the world's values and goals.

In its local setting all the principles of the universal church find practical and pragmatic expression. A local congregation can be seen as they serve one another and the local community. It is in the local church that Christians are motivated and equipped to live the life of Christ, and not just in the church but in the marketplaces of daily life. Furthermore, the local church is at the sharp end of proclaiming the gospel – the good news of who Jesus is and what he said and did.

For the local church to be all of this it needs to be strategic.

So what makes a church strategic? For starters, let's use the word 'strategic' to remind us of some important principles involved in building a strategic church:

Strong Leadership
Team Spirit
Relational Structures
Application Preaching
Training and Equipping of Lay Leadership
Exponential Thinking
Generous Attitude
Innovative Involvement with the Local Community
Caring Heart

Throughout the coming chapters we shall look at these principles more closely.

The goal is a healthy church. A good strategy is not just to increase the numerical size of the church. Some of the emphasis of the church growth movement has concentrated too much on numerical growth. A good strategy for church growth focuses on the spiritual health of the church. It keeps in mind that exhortation of St Paul to be 'like-minded, having the same love, being one in spirit and purpose' (Philippians 2:2).

No church, of course, is perfect, any more than any physical human body is perfect, but it can be healthy in that it is being and doing what Jesus Christ would have us be and do – what some have described as a fully functioning, Holy Spirit-led church. The best description of spiritual health is found in Galatians 5:22–23, 'But when the Holy Spirit controls our lives, he will produce this kind of fruit in us: love, joy, peace, patience, kindness, goodness, faithfulness, gentleness, and self-control' (NLT).

Which brings us back to the foundational principle we began with: only God can make the church grow, but there are things that he expects us to do. Remember that principle is summed up in 1 Corinthians 3:6, where the apostle Paul says, concerning the church in Corinth, 'I planted the seed, Apollos watered it, but God made it grow.' Here we see our part and God's part. Our part is to focus on the health of a local Christian community. God promises to take care of the growth.

One word can sum up our part – intentionality.

Intentionality involves developing a clear strategy for connecting people with Jesus Christ, discipling them, and equipping them for service and mission. This calls for an intentional strategy that will include prayer, a total dependence on the Holy Spirit, an openness to God's purposes and a readiness to use today's technology and language to present the good news of Jesus Christ to a world searching for peace.

Let's now unpack this noble task step by step.

2

Strong Leadership

D r Sam Keen, a well-known professor of philosophy and religion, said that a wise person is someone 'who knows what time it is' in their own life and in the history around them. To put that another way, if we do not understand the time in which we live, we will not be understood ourselves. Wise leaders know 'what time it is' in their own lives and in the institutions or movements they lead. A strategic church is a church that knows 'what time it is' in their church and in their community.

> New-paradigm churches have a leadership that recognises the centrality of worship and emphasises a transformational encounter with the living God. Their leaders are concerned with equipping the people of God for mission in the world. They are committed to identifying, training, granting peer support to and mentoring their fellow leaders. They empower emerging leaders and are ambitious for them. Leaders of new-paradigm churches are accessible and vulnerable.[1]

Whether it is paid or unpaid, trained or untrained, strong servant leadership is the catalyst of a healthy, growing church. Everything rises or falls on servant leadership, however small or large the church may be. As the Christian community takes on new shapes

---

[1] Eddie Gibbs and Ian Coffey, *Church Next*, IVP 2001, p. 230.

and expressions of being church, there are timeless New Testament values and principles that leaders, particularly vocational leaders, need to implement. Regrettably, such values and principles have frequently been compromised by cultural expectations. For example, back in the 1970s the church growth department of the Bible Society published a list of 14 different expectations by congregations placed upon the average minister. These were:

1. Visiting
2. Teaching
3. Counselling
4. Administration
5. Evangelism
6. Team leadership
7. Training
8. Community leadership
9. Congregational leadership
10. Personal development and in-service training
11. Denominational and ecumenical responsibilities
12. Leading worship
13. Enabling
14. Sacramental and priestly functions

The end result of these expectations was to place the entire responsibility for what the church should be and do on the shoulders of the individual minister.

It was concluded by many regional church leaders – superintendents, moderators and bishops – that any one minister would not be sufficiently gifted or able adequately to satisfy more than three or four of these expectations of leadership. In many churches the result was, and in some churches still is, frustration on the part of both congregation and minister.

So where should the emphasis be? What do servant-hearted Christian leaders look like?

Sustained by God

They are sustained by God. In other words, they have an over-whelming sense of dependence upon God. They exercise this dependence on a daily basis. They rely entirely upon God for their strength – spiritually, emotionally and physically. They spend time alone with God. They know that 'Unless the Lord builds the house, its builders labour in vain' (Psalm 127:1).

The point is that God sustains strong, effective and authentic leaders because they choose to live that way.

Such leaders follow the example of Jesus, who took time to be alone with his Father. In John's Gospel Jesus summed up this indispensable dependence:

> Remain in me, and I will remain in you. No branch can bear fruit by itself; it must remain in the vine. Neither can you bear fruit unless you remain in me. I am the vine; you are the branches. If you remain in me and I in you, you will bear much fruit: apart from me you can do nothing. (John 15:4–5 NIV Incl.)

We need to be connected.

> If you remain in me and my words remain in you, ask whatever you wish, and it will be given you. This is to my Father's glory that you bear much fruit, showing yourselves to be my disciples. (John 15:7–8)

There is nothing vague about this.

Clearly, a leader's relationship with God is essential. Every-thing depends on this relationship. The New Testament reminds us of this truth over and over again. The apostle Paul writes, 'I can do everything through him [Christ] who gives me strength' (Philippians 4:13).

Over the years my dependence on God has varied, and I am sure I am not alone in this. Sometimes I have found it difficult to know what total dependence on God really means. Sometimes I have felt very dependent, and other times I know I have taken control. The fine line between dependence on God and doing what God expects me to do, using the gifts he has given me, has not always been clear. However, this is probably true even for those leaders I admire and look to as examples of closeness to God. But they have been convinced that such dependence is essential.

Spurgeon once said,

> Dependence on God is the flowing fountain of success. That true saint of God, George Muller, has always struck me, when I have heard him speak, as being such a simple, child-like being in his dependence upon God; but alas! Most of us are far too great for God to use us; we can preach as well as anybody, make a sermon with anybody – and so we fail. Take care, brethren, for if we think we can do anything of ourselves, all we shall get from God is the opportunity to try.[2]

A strong leader who is self-sufficient is a danger to any church.

Tell their story

Servant leaders are ready to tell the story of their journey with God, not in a superior manner but in the candid way in which the apostle Paul told the story of his meeting with Christ (Acts 22, 26).

Leaders need to be transparent. People need to know their leaders have a real relationship with God. They want to know whether they are authentic followers of Christ. They want to know not only that the message is trustworthy, but that the messenger is trustworthy as well.

The story of a leader's relationship with God can be a strong and persuasive influence. It was said of Spurgeon,

> Mr. Spurgeon played his part well in the practical world, but his life was not there. The growth of the kingdom of grace was his prosperity.

---

[2] Larry Michael, *Spurgeon on Leadership*, Kregel 2003, p. 38.

This spirituality is so rare in men of great powers that it is invariably the way to influence. It inspires a kind of awe. Men bow before it, feel themselves in the presence of the eternal world, think wistfully of their own state, and are touched for a moment at least by a certain sense of wonder and regret.[3]

I can think of other leaders of whom similar observations have been made – leaders as different as Mother Teresa and Billy Graham.

It was his close relationship with the Father that caused the disciples to ask Jesus the question, 'Lord, teach us to pray' (Luke 11:1). What the disciples wanted at that point was not so much an academic teaching on how to pray but how to build a closer relationship with God. Jesus gave his answer by giving what we have come to know as the Lord's Prayer.

People need to be able to see into the heart of the leader. Leaders who can share their own sense of vulnerability encourage others to be honest. Hopefully, gone are the days when church ministers were perceived to be 6 feet above their congregation. Christian leaders are just as vulnerable as secular leaders. The Bible gives us a clear warning: 'So, if you think you are standing firm, be careful that you don't fall!' (1 Corinthians 10:12).

People need to know that leaders experience many of the same trials and temptations that those they lead experience. If leaders are preaching on the fruit of the Spirit, 'love, joy, peace, patience, kindness, goodness, faithfulness, gentleness and self-control' (Galatians 5:22–23), they need to be honest enough to say how they are progressing with this list of qualities and Christlikeness. Leaders will have stories about how they are learning patience or wishing they were doing better with self-control. They may have a story about how God taught them certain qualities of character through difficult stretches of life. When I have asked my congregation,

---

[3] Sir W. Robertson Nicoll (ed.), *Introduction to Sermons by Revd C. H. Spurgeon*, Thomas Nelson & Sons 1900, pp. 9, 10.

'How are you getting on with "gentleness"?' I have admitted, 'I struggle with that sometimes.' That kind of admission can encourage and motivate people on their own spiritual journey.

All authentic Christians, including leaders, have more than one testimony or story to tell that will help others. Some people believe that Christian leaders do not have the same problems as anyone else, and this is due in part to leaders who want to project a certain image of themselves or who have never taken the time publicly to admit their learning experiences, their struggles or their vulnerability. This has nothing to do with wearing your heart on your sleeve: it is about the strength of meekness, honesty and genuine humility.

Relate to each other

One of the signs of strong servant leadership is the desire and ability to build healthy relationships. The apostle Paul said,

> I make myself a slave to everyone, to win as many as possible. To the Jews I became like a Jew, to win the Jews. To those under the law I became like one under the law . . . so as to win those under the law. (1 Corinthians 9:19–20)

> To the weak I became weak, to win the weak. I have become all things to all men so that by all possible means I might save some. (1 Corinthians 9:22)

Paul's desire to build healthy relationships is also seen in his wish to visit the Christians in Rome. 'I long to see you so that I may impart to you some spiritual gift to make you strong – that is, that you and I may be mutually encouraged by each other's faith' (Romans 1:11–12).

Building relationships is another basic principle that we may struggle with. The demands of church leadership are sometimes such that the very last thing you want to do is relate to people. 'I just want a break from people,' one pastor said to me. 'I'm all peopled out,' said another. So once again we are talking about essential principles that are not always easy to practise, sometimes depending on your personal temperament. Are you introvert or extrovert?

Some leaders very much enjoy being on the stage. They love to lead in worship. They love to preach, they love to teach, inspire and encourage, but all from a distance. They don't really want to spend time with individuals. If they could lead a church without having to get involved in the lives of individual people, they would be very happy. Before long that kind of attitude becomes apparent to people in the church and is the exact opposite of good leadership. It is possible to impress people from a distance, but you will influence them most when you are close to them.

Focus on developing and shaping people, not just on imparting knowledge. Don't focus on simply getting through the lesson, but on helping people grow.

'The Christian leader who ministers effectively to his followers understands that pastoral care has to be a priority. It is really about nurturing relationships.'[4]

Obedient to God

Obedience to God is another key component of strong leadership. No amount of planning and vision-casting will make up for lack of obedience to God. If we are to be all that God wants us to be, and if the church is to be all that God wants the church to be, then we must follow him. We are disciples. When Jesus gave what we call the Great Commission, he said to the first disciples that they were to go and make other disciples of all nations, 'teaching them to obey everything I have commanded you' (Matthew 28:20). Obedience to Christ is an essential quality of discipleship.

---

[4] Larry Michael, *Spurgeon on Leadership*, Kregel 2003, p. 155.

One of the huge temptations of leadership is to try to please as many people as possible. At times most of us have fallen into this attractive snare, even though we know full well that it is a recipe for disaster. While, humanly speaking, we do desire to please people, we want our priority to be always to please God. Happily that sometimes results in pleasing others as well.

Tom Landry, the well-known Dallas Cowboys football coach mentioned previously, puts it like this: 'Leadership is getting someone to do what they don't want to do, to achieve what they want to achieve.'

Whenever we try to lead by pleasing others we nearly always end up with division. The moment you please one group of people, you immediately disappoint another group. Someone said that 'the art of leadership is the management of disappointment'.

Strategic Christian leadership begins at the cross of Jesus Christ. It is said of Billy Graham, one of the most strategic Christian leaders of the twentieth century, that his 'leadership has always been in the context of what he understood Jesus to have endured to bring others peace and hope, and what he himself must endure to communicate that message'.[5]

Sherwood Wirt, long-time editor of Billy's *Decision* magazine, observed, 'All attempts to explain Billy Graham fail unless they begin at the cross'. Billy often reflected on the words of Jesus to his disciples, 'If any of you wants to be my follower', he told them, 'you must put aside your selfish ambition, shoulder your cross, and follow me. If you try keep your life for yourself you will lose it but if you give up your life for my sake and for the sake of the good news, you will find true life' (Mark 8:34–35 NLT). Billy denied himself in countless ways and took up his cross and followed Jesus.[6]

---

[5] Harold Myra and Marshall Shelley, *The Leadership Secrets of Billy Graham*, Zondervan 2005, p. 31.

[6] *Ibid.*, pp. 31–32.

Strong leaders need to be strong followers.

Obedience to God also includes obedience to his character. Strong leaders know the difference between giftedness and character. Strength of character is needed to overcome life's temptations. Strong leaders are men and women of total integrity. Such leadership is needed in our world today in all areas of life where, because of the influence of the mass media, people no longer know the difference between celebrities and leaders.

The leader who places obedience to God at the top of his or her agenda is the person who, in the long term, finds the greatest fulfilment, even though there is pain in resisting the temptation to please everyone.

Nurture others

To nurture is to encourage the development of others. This is one of the key tasks of leadership. We nurture others by affirming them, by offering encouragement and opportunities for spiritual and emotional growth. The most effective and influential Christian leaders are those who have spent time nurturing others.

Nurturing is not just a function. It is also an attitude. The leader notices what is happening in people's lives. Leaders nurture others in a number of different ways. Those who are close to the leader will be nurtured one-on-one. We remember that Jesus spent time with his twelve disciples. They benefited from his teaching them and nurturing them and developing them. Jesus also nurtured those he met perhaps just once, such as the Samaritan woman he met at the well, mentioned in John 4; and also people like Nicodemus and Zacchaeus, and others, with whom he had less time than he did with the disciples. But Jesus took every opportunity to speak on an individual basis with anybody. He affirmed and encouraged and challenged those he met. Jesus also nurtured the crowds: 'The large crowd listened to him with delight' (Mark 12:37). We remember the way in which he provided for over five thousand people who listened to him for so long that they became hungry. He nurtured them by providing for them both spiritually and physically. In the same way there are times when leaders will nurture individuals, those closest to them, including their fellow leaders and team members. Then there are occasions when the leader will nurture the crowd. And that too must never be underestimated in terms of importance and influence.

What does nurturing look like?

Jesus not only taught the disciples, but also opened up opportunities for them. He sent them out two by two to put into practice what he had been teaching them. When we follow this example of Jesus' we are inevitably taking risks, but people grow through their mistakes, even as the disciples grew through their mistakes and times of apparent failure.

The apostle Paul is a great example of nurturing not only fellow leaders but also entire churches. For example, when he writes to the Christians in Rome, he says:

> First, I thank my God through Jesus Christ for all of you, because your faith is being reported all over the world. God, whom I serve with my whole heart in preaching the gospel of his Son, is my witness how constantly I remember you in my prayers at all times; and I pray that now at last by God's will the way may be opened for me to come to you. I long to see you so that I may impart to you some spiritual gift to make you strong – that is, that you and I may be mutually encouraged by each other's faith. (Romans 1:8–12)

Part of nurturing is about challenging people, and even though Paul challenged the church at Corinth when he wrote to them, he began his letter by saying:

> I always thank God for you because of his grace given you in Christ Jesus. For in him you have been enriched in every way – in all your

speaking and in all your knowledge – because our testimony about Christ was confirmed in you. Therefore you do not lack any spiritual gift as you eagerly wait for our Lord Jesus Christ to be revealed. He will keep you strong to the end, so that you will be blameless on the day of our Lord Jesus Christ. God, who has called you into fellowship with his Son Jesus Christ our Lord, is faithful. (1 Corinthians 1:4–9)

Paul was affirming and encouraging:

We always thank God, the Father of our Lord Jesus Christ, when we pray for you, because we have heard of your faith in Christ Jesus and of the love you have for all the saints – the faith and love that spring from the hope that is stored up for you in heaven and that you have already heard about in the word of truth, the gospel that has come to you. All over the world this gospel is bearing fruit and growing, just as it has been doing among you since the day you heard it and understood God's grace in all its truth. (Colossians 1:3–6)

And again in 1 Thessalonians 1:2–3:

We always thank God for all of you, mentioning you in our prayers. We continually remember before our God and Father your work produced by faith, your labour prompted by love, and your endurance inspired by hope in our Lord Jesus Christ.

And in 2 Thessalonians 1: 3–4:

We ought always to thank God for you, brothers, and rightly so, because your faith is growing more and more, and the love every one of you has for each other is increasing. Therefore, among God's churches we boast about your perseverance and faith in all the persecutions and trials you are enduring.

Nurturing others can be anything from taking the time to stop and say a brief word of encouragement or affirmation to more formal times of nurturing through the teaching and training of individuals and small groups. It is a joy to see how people grow, open up and develop through words of affirmation, encouragement and challenge.

By now you may be asking, 'Where do we find the time to do this?' Nurturing does not necessarily mean we spend huge amounts of personal time with individuals. Sometimes it may require that, but there are times when we nurture in other ways:

> Many of those heavily influenced by Billy [Graham] spend little one on one time with him. Jay [Kesler] says that despite relatively few in-person meetings 'Billy has been huge for me. He embodied what we wanted to emulate.' Jay, a voracious reader of thoughtful books, and a brilliant communicator, has very different capacities from Billy. Yet like many leaders with the same core commitments, he saw in Billy integrity, wisdom, and the flag he could follow.[7]

The attitude of nurturing can be contagious, and if caught by the entire team, then the whole organisation can provide tremendous encouragement for and be a great influence on others, usually because they have a shared vision. An example of this is when an entire church, small or mega, is an environment of encouragement and affirmation.

Nurturing is long term with regard to those immediately around you, and sometimes to those who are more distant. It's keeping track of them over a length of time. It's remembering their vision when they themselves have forgotten it. Someone can live a very long time off a word of encouragement or affirmation that you have given them.

Generous to everyone

If someone is self-absorbed, obsessed with building their own empire and keeping everything for themselves, they are not likely to attract many followers. Obviously, if you are not attracting followers, you are not a leader. As is often said, just look over your shoulder, and if there is no one there, you're probably not a leader.

---

[7] *Ibid.*, p. 241.

The most effective and influential leaders are normally generous with their time, their energy and their resources. There are many examples, but one is probably sufficient. Sir John Laing, a world-renowned builder, made and gave away a vast fortune. A strong leader in his field, thousands benefited from his generosity well beyond the limits of his organisation. He was often encouraged by others to live in a much bigger house than the one he had. His response was, 'Everyone should have a house just big enough to serve its purpose, as to have more than that causes such a lot of work.'[8] His biographer, Roy Coad, says, 'On another occasion he declined a Rolls Royce car that his family wished to present to him: he preferred to stay with the Rover that in later life he always used.' Yet Laing was generous in his attitude and never spoke disparagingly of those who did live more ostentatiously. Even as early as the 1940s he had been giving away £20,000 a year, many times the modest income he retained for himself.[9] 'In April 1978, after his death, his net estate was published at £371. The man who had handled millions had given them all away.'[10]

Sir John Laing demonstrated generosity in other ways. He never bore a grudge. He did not harbour resentment. He was peace-loving and tolerant, yet at the same time he was very determined and intentional in what he accomplished.

A very powerful truth emerges from the story of Sir John Laing. He was a medium-sized, gently spoken man who did not have a strong physical presence, apart from his winning smile. In these days leadership is often equated with physical appearance or size. Sir John's story proves that leadership has nothing to do with either of these. Leadership supremely is influence. Sir John was generous of heart and spirit. Like many others before him, in

---

[8] Roy Coad, *Laing*, Hodder and Stoughton 1979, p. 210.

[9] *Ibid.*, p. 213.   [10] *Ibid.*, p. 215.

his own generation and ever since, he followed the example of Jesus Christ in his magnanimity. Jesus is the most magnanimous person who ever lived.

Lead by leading

For a variety of reasons, leaders do not always lead. There are occasions when they shy away from the responsibilities of leadership and hide behind others. How often we hear it said, 'They are supposed to be the leader: why don't they take the lead?' For some, it is a case of never having developed their leadership skills. Although many leaders are gifted, those gifts need to be honed and developed, and much of leadership is learned. Leadership can lay latent in a person for years before it is identified, if ever.

One of the key factors in leading is building and energising a team. The very nature of leadership means you cannot lead in isolation. It is also obvious that no one person can do everything. Not even Jesus could meet the needs of all the people of his day, and so he built and relied on a team. A strong strategic leader will always build a team. Whether one is leading a large enterprise or church or a small organisation, teamwork multiplies effectiveness.

One of the key secrets to mobilising a strong team is to articulate a compelling vision. A compelling vision unites the team, and it all starts with the leader. As already mentioned, everything stands or falls on leadership.

Taking the lead is not always easy. Darren Blaney, a Baptist minister writing in the *Baptist Times* under the heading 'Why our churches don't want leaders', says that 'despite all rhetoric to the contrary, many churches appear extremely reluctant to be led into significant change'. He goes on to say, 'Our churches may not want leaders, but they desperately need them.'

When one is faced with people who do not want to be led,

particular challenges of leadership arise. Often the temptation is to back down, but a strategic leader will not give up. Instead he or she will find a way through. I repeat a statement by Tom Landry: 'Leadership is getting someone to do what they don't want to do, to achieve what they want to achieve.'

It may seem obvious to say that leaders should lead, but there are times when we abdicate. Churches and leaders that have a congregational structure of government, particularly in the UK, are nervous about strong leadership. But many of those churches are in urgent need of strong visionary servant leadership.

I remember being challenged early on in my own ministry, when a fellow church leader of my church came to me and said, 'This church doesn't have a team leader any more.' I realised that I was shirking the responsibility of leadership. The temptations to back away, give up or give in are many. This doesn't mean we do not make mistakes or cover our weaknesses, as we shall see later in this chapter.

Leaders need the resolve of the apostles:

> It would not be right for us to neglect the ministry of the word of God in order to wait on tables. Brothers and sisters, choose seven men from among you who are known to be full of the Spirit and wisdom. We will turn this responsibility over to them and will give our attention to prayer and the ministry of the word. (Acts 6:2–4 NIV Incl.)

The result of this was 'the word of God spread. The number of disciples in Jerusalem increased rapidly, and a large number of priests became obedient to the faith' (Acts 6:7). That passage of scripture is an encouraging example of leaders who lead. They are not side-tracked to other tasks, even though there is a need, but they find a way through the problem and see whether there's an opportunity for further growth. Through their leadership they free up the enterprise so that it continues to grow.

Encourage

'We have different gifts according to the grace given us'; 'if it is encouraging, then encourage' (Romans 12:6, 8 NIV Incl.). The gift of encouragement has great influence. Acts 4 mentions a man called Joseph, a Levite from Cyprus. He was nicknamed 'Barnabas', which means 'son of encouragement'. Of course encouragement is a gift not limited to those in the leadership. There are many in our congregations who have the gift of encouragement. These are people who stand out from the crowd and frequently encourage leaders. In fact, leaders draw inspiration from them. In total contrast, discouragement can be very damaging to the unity and health of the church. So there is good reason for everybody to be encouraging, even though they may not stand out as having the gift of encouragement.

A pastor or senior minister may not necessarily have the gift of encouragement and may not be the one who stands out as the 'encourager' of the congregation. However, a leader who does not encourage others is severely weakened in his or her influence of leadership. The word 'encouragement' is mentioned many times in the New Testament and is a quality that every leader needs to cultivate. How often I have heard people say of a leader, 'He (or she) is so encouraging.' All effective, strong, strategic Christian leaders have been men and women of enormous encouragement to others. It doesn't actually take a lot of time and energy to encourage others.

Admit your own limitations

Leaders need to face up to their own vulnerability. The Bible spells it out very clearly when it says, 'So, if you think you are standing firm, be careful that you don't fall' (1 Corinthians 10:12). The best leaders are painfully aware of their humanity.

Accepting our human limitations, including our personal weaknesses, is crucial to authenticity. This is where we need other team members. This is where we need accountability. A leader who doesn't admit to weaknesses has no need for team-mates.

To admit our weaknesses and our mistakes and failures is not a sign of weakness: it is a sign of hope. We remember the admonition of the Bible when it says that in our weaknesses we are strong.

This doesn't mean that we should continually be reminding people of our sinfulness. There are those who appear to be proud of their weaknesses and their mistakes and failures. There is a time and a place to admit to these things. We also need to bear in mind that there are some people who find it difficult to handle the weaknesses of leaders. Leaders should not place on others a burden that is very difficult for them to bear. Often it is a case of building an environment of acceptance and a culture of forgiveness where people sense the freedom to be open and honest with each other. And so there comes a moment when it is right for a leader to say, 'I made a mistake' or 'I'm sorry' or 'I struggle with this particular issue.'

> This openness should never be allowed to degenerate into a display of one's sin before the whole world just for the sake of the display. Some have fallen into this demonic trap. Such an exercise can become very damaging to spiritual health and fellowship. Nor should we engage in a morbid inner search to dredge up old sins. Such introspection does not bring about spiritual health; rather, it precipitates spiritual sickness. Moreover, there are some areas of our lives about which only God should ever know.[11]

Admitting our weaknesses and mistakes actually helps us to deal with our critics.

---

[11] Lewis A. Drummond, *Eight Keys to Spiritual Revival*, Bethany House Publishers 1994, p. 95.

All leaders get criticised. It's your response to criticism that sets you apart. The great Victorian preacher Charles Haddon Spurgeon, who was frequently criticised, said this:

> Get a friend to tell you your faults or, better still, welcome an enemy who will watch you keenly and sting you savagely. What a blessing such an irritating critic will be to a wise man.

Leaders do well not to take themselves too seriously. Leaders tell stories against themselves. A theological college principal once told his students how he was preaching one Sunday morning when, after he had got ten minutes into the sermon, someone stood up at the back of the congregation and called out, 'Come on: get to the point!' It takes courage to tell stories against yourself.

Having nurtured and encouraged others, leaders then need to:

Delegate to set people free

This includes not only the delegation of tasks but also the delegation of authority. If a leader is not a team player, then the leader will find it very difficult to delegate. Delegation inevitably involves trust. A leader who can delegate will share with another person the big picture and will describe the task that needs to be accomplished, but will then leave that person with the details.

A leader with a large vision knows it will not be accomplished without selecting the right people who can be trusted to implement the vision with authority. Delegation means giving clear guidance but also freedom to implement the task in hand. It not only means trust in the other person, it means respecting and highly valuing them. It means giving them credit and praise when they do their work well. Most people need to feel appreciated, and their confidence needs to be built up. The task of delegation is to challenge and inspire others. It is fulfilling to watch others fulfil their potential.

Delegation is a way of unleashing the talents, skills and gifts of others. It is not only about empowering others, it is also about being ready to accept their failures, which are inevitable in the learning process. A leader's responsibility is to unlock the potential of others and to respect and nurture that potential. Eventually delegation will free up not only the individual but also the leader. Bill Gates, Chairman and Chief Software Architect of Microsoft, once said, 'The notion that things have to come through me just goes back to people just not understanding how things really work here. There's an incredible number of people making autonomous decisions.'[12] The great evangelist Dwight L. Moody once said, 'I'd rather get ten men to do the right job than to do the job of ten men.' Some pastors and church leaders want to keep things to themselves and want to know every detail of what happens, even after they have delegated the responsibility to someone else. Sometimes they find it difficult actually to let go of control.

Control is often a very big issue in the church. Every pastor and church leader must decide whether they will structure the church for control or structure it for growth. If a church is structured for control, it will eventually stifle the creativity of its members, restrict the growth of the church itself and create a lot of frustration. This kind of structure also sets the church up for lots of meetings.

To give up control is not always easy. Some leaders dislike the feeling of being out of control. It feels risky. It calls for a step of faith. It doesn't mean there is no accountability. It's just that accountability is handled in a different way.

Delegation sets people free for ministry. It sets them free from meetings and committees. 'Most churches are not structured for the laity to do ministry. Persons involved in the church often

---

[12] Bill Gates, as quoted in *BusinessWeek Online*, 19th June 2006.

spend their time on committees or boards rather than in frontline ministry.'[13]

Equip others for service

Equipping others is another key role of leadership. This is clearly explained in the Bible:

> It was he who gave some to be apostles, some to be prophets, some to be evangelists, and some to be pastors and teachers, to prepare God's people for works of service, so that the body of Christ may be built up until we all reach unity in the faith and in the knowledge of the Son of God and become mature, attaining to the whole measure of the fulness of Christ. (Ephesians 4:11–13)

Notice that the task of equipping others is not the responsibility of just one leader, but a group of leaders. There are five leadership roles mentioned, and together they form a group that is to 'prepare God's people for works of service'.

> There is a great deal in the Bible about leadership. Two points are vital here: First, the Bible assumes that one person will not be given all the gifts required to create a healthy community. Second, the Bible makes it clear that the role of leaders, whatever their particular talents, is to equip and grow people in character and godly service.[14]

Equipping others involves more than nurturing and delegating. Equipping also means providing the tools to do the job. Church members sometimes believe they are delegated to tasks but are often ill-equipped to do them. Members of the Christian community involved in the life and ministry of the local church need supporting, not only through encouragement and spiritual input but also by providing practical support and material sources and tools.

---

[13] Thom Rainer, *A Book of Church Growth*, Broadman 1993, p. 200.

[14] Mark Greene and Tracey Cotterell, *Let My People Grow*, LICC 2005, p.13.

How often we hear of workers, such as children's workers, who feel they have not got the tools and materials they need to do the job.

Release and let go

One of my previous books was entitled *Releasing Your Church to Grow*. This brings us back to the issue of control. Over the centuries Christians have discovered that they cannot control the church, no matter how hard they try nor how far they seem to succeed. Jesus said, 'I will build my church', and we need to allow him to do just that. The evangelist Charles Finney used to say that it is up to each generation to discover which way the Holy Spirit is moving and then follow.

Part of releasing the church to grow means that we need to release those we are leading. It means that we show each other grace. We let go, and we treat others the same as Jesus treats us. Without exactly encouraging people to make mistakes, we need to allow them to make mistakes and recognise that mistakes will happen. Obviously, there has to be accountability. Perhaps the best illustration is that of a parent and child. The parent cannot make the child grow, but the parent can provide the environment in which the child can grow. Sometimes that means allowing the child to learn through making mistakes. In 2 Corinthians 11:1, the apostle Paul says, 'I hope you will be patient with me' (NLT).

Sometimes others do not grow because of lack of confidence or fear. Dr Rowan Williams, the Archbishop of Canterbury, said at Spring Harvest in the UK in 2006 that he was 'hopeful, but not optimistic' about the British church. He went on to say,

> the most important thing for Christians to pray for is for God to take away our fear. What comes across from Christians very often is fear rather than trust. But if the message that we give is that we are anxious all the time, it doesn't feel like good news.[15]

---

[15] *Christianity* magazine, June 2006, p. 10.

A leader's responsibility is to release others from fear and to build their confidence, to let them know that it is not the end of the world when they make mistakes, and that in fact until they do make mistakes they may not learn.

Releasing others means delegating responsibility and keeping accountability, and letting folk go and do the job that they have been called to do. It means leaders taking their hands off the details and releasing fellow leaders and other workers to do their work. Releasing others to grow sometimes means the willingness to experiment and even to fail, but to use failures as a means of learning for the future.

Part of releasing is recognising that people learn in different ways. Some people learn through books; some are more visual; others learn through discussion; others again learn through experience. People learn in a variety of ways, and not only should the local church provide these different ways to enable them to learn, but the leadership has a responsibility to release the people to grow in the way that is best suited to them.

As we release individual people to grow, we are releasing the whole community to grow. We need to build a healthy recognition that everybody is in the process of growing and learning. We are all apprentices on the road to discipleship.

When thinking of releasing the church and the individuals within it to grow, we are reminded of the old definition of a saint: 'someone who has learnt to get out of God's way'.

Safeguard others against compromise

A strategic Christian leader will safeguard others as well as him- or herself. Today's world is full of temptations. There are not only the blatantly obvious temptations that surround us, but also the more subtle ones that can weaken our effectiveness or lead us into greater compromise. It seems that the more effective the

Christian leader is, the greater the temptations to compromise. The temptations to compromise usually centre around the old issues of pride, sexual immorality, questionable handling of money, jealousy of others' success and exaggerated accomplishments. Safeguarding oneself means an honest recognition of one's own weaknesses and the particular areas of temptation. This needs to be followed by structures of accountability. Safeguarding others may involve extending the accountability structures to other members of the team. The Billy Graham team did this very effectively early on in their ministry. 'By openly declaring their ethical standards, the Graham team admitted the dangers and clarified the expectations.'[16]

The team produced a manifesto:

• We will never criticise, condemn or speak negatively about others.
• We will be accountable, particularly in handling finances, within integrity – according to the highest business standards.
• We will tell the truth and be thoroughly honest, especially in reporting statistics.
• We will be exemplary in morals – clear, clean and careful to avoid the very appearance of any impropriety.[17]

Many other Christian leaders have followed the example of the Billy Graham team, including Rick Warren, pastor of Saddleback Community Church in Orange County, California, and the members of his team.

Part of the practice of safeguarding others includes being unwilling to divulge confidences. There may be times when not betraying a confidence compounds a problematic situation, compromising other ethical and moral principles. In such instances

---

[16] Harold Myra and Marshall Shelley, *The Leadership Secrets of Billy Graham,* Zondervan 2005, p. 61.   [17] *Ibid.*

there may be a price to pay, including being misunderstood. There are times when a leader can easily justify him- or herself simply by betraying a confidence. None of us is perfect. Everyone fails at some point, and there are times when we need others around to stand up for us.

'But among you there must not be even a hint of sexual immorality, or of any kind of impurity, or of greed, because these are improper for God's holy people' (Ephesians 5:3). If you are a leader, put the safeguards in place.

Harmonise for unity and purpose

One of the key commands of the New Testament is to 'make every effort to keep the unity of the Spirit' (Ephesians 4:3). The same instruction is mentioned in Philippians 2:2: 'Make my joy complete by being like-minded, having the same love, being one in spirit and purpose.' Unity of purpose is high on the agenda of the New Testament.

Whatever size a church may be, whether it is a traditional model or a new expression of church, this principle of unity of purpose is central to Christian life and community. Without unity of purpose churches have been weakened not only in their fellowship together but also in the effectiveness of their mission. Sadly, much could be written about arguments, disagreements and divisions within the Christian community.

Keeping the unity of the Spirit does not mean that we necessarily all agree on everything. God has made us all different, and we need to recognise those differences. But, 'Be kind and compassionate to one another, forgiving each other, just as in Christ God forgave you' (Ephesians 4:32). Unity of purpose is most important, rather than everyone agreeing on secondary issues that do not affect the purpose of the church.

Inspire your people

When Jesus first called the disciples to follow him, there was something about him that inspired them.

As Jesus walked beside the Sea of Galilee, he saw Simon and his brother Andrew casting a net into the lake, for they were fishermen. 'Come, follow me,' Jesus said, 'and I will make you fishers of men.' At once they left their nets and followed him. (Mark 1:16–18)

Jesus inspired, as well as challenging and rebuking. What was it that made Zacchaeus say, 'Look, Lord! Here and now I give half of my possessions to the poor, and if I have cheated anybody out of anything, I will pay back four times the amount' (Luke 19:8)?

When Jesus gave the disciples the Great Commission (Matthew 28:19), he was not only challenging, he was also inspiring and casting a vision for their lives. When he appears to them again, he refines the vision and inspires them once more. 'But you will receive power when the Holy Spirit comes on you; and you will be my witnesses in Jerusalem, and in all Judea and Samaria, and to the ends of the earth' (Acts 1:8).

'Effective leaders are able to create and sustain a compelling vision for their followers.'[18] Strategic, godly leaders get their vision from God. Knowing that it is from God, they then have the capacity to inspire others to be part of it.

Inspiring others, however, is not always easy. For example, William Carey, described as the father of modern missions, had to overcome enormous difficulty to inspire people to see the needs of India. When he shared his vision with fellow ministers at a Baptist fraternal in Northamptonshire, he was told, 'Sit down, young man. You're an enthusiast.' John Wesley effectively inspired people and became the founder of Methodism. C. H. Spurgeon, having received his vision from God, led a declining

---

[18] Larry Michael, *Spurgeon on Leadership*, Kregel 2003, p. 91.

church in the heart of London to renewed growth and service, eventually reaching thousands of people with the gospel of Christ. A modern-day example of inspiring others is the ministry of Rick Warren. At the first worship service of the Saddleback Community Church, Rick shared a vision that we shall look at in more detail later, but it had the power to be compellingly inspiring to the first members of the Saddleback Church, and still is so today, when that church is having an influence across the whole world.

Purposely unite your team

An inspiring and compelling vision comes only from leaders who are purposeful. Without purpose, people do purposeless things, and that includes some leaders. Without a sense of purpose, a leader is going nowhere, and neither will he or she be able to lead others towards a goal. Without a sense of purpose within the Christian community, everyone will make up their own, and they will follow the purpose that seems right in their own eyes. This creates disunity and frustration. Purpose brings about the exact opposite. It unites people.

Alongside this book on strategy, I strongly recommend that readers study the books *The Purpose Driven Life* and *The Purpose Driven Church* (see Bibliography, p. 215).

People will follow a person of purpose. Jesus had a strong sense of purpose as he began his ministry and as eventually he journeyed to Jerusalem and the cross. The apostle Paul had a strong sense of purpose throughout the whole of his ministry, and when he writes from a prison cell to the Christians in Philippi, his letter breathes purpose from start to finish, so much so that other issues are set aside in his mind – even the competitiveness of other preachers. He has no resentment or jealousy in his heart as he writes:

> Now I want you to know, brothers, that what has happened to me has really served to advance the gospel. (Philippians 1:12)

> It is true that some preach Christ out of envy and rivalry but others out of goodwill. The latter do so in love, knowing that I am put here for the defence of the gospel. The former preach Christ out of selfish ambition, not sincerely, supposing that they can stir up trouble for me while I am in chains. But what does is matter? The important thing is that in every way, whether from false motives or true, Christ is preached. And because of this I rejoice. (Philippians 1:15–18)

'How can I implement all this?' may be your question as you come to the end of this chapter. Answer: one step at a time. That is the way to approach the coming chapters as well. Remember the counsel mentioned in the first chapter:

> For this very reason, make every effort to add to your faith goodness; and to goodness, knowledge; and to knowledge, self-control; and to self-control, perseverance; and to perseverance, godliness; and to godliness, mutual affection; and to mutual affection, love. (2 Peter 1:5–7 NIV Incl.)

In other words, one step at a time. That's the strategy for personal growth!

In the coming chapters, let us look at how strategic leaders can build strategic churches.

3

Team Spirit

B uilding a strategic church is a team effort. Ephesians 4:11–12 describes a team:

> It was he who gave some to be apostles, some to be prophets, some to be evangelists, and some to be pastors and teachers, to prepare God's people for works of service, so that the body of Christ may be built up.

These verses not only describe a team but also spell out the fact that a healthy church is the result of a team working together. It takes a whole team to build a healthy strategic church.

One of the best examples of a wholesome team spirit is the Billy Graham team, which has stayed together for approximately half a century. Rick Warren, Pastor of the Saddleback Community Church in Orange County, California, writes:

> Billy and his team have been the model of teamwork for our leadership team at Saddleback. We intentionally modeled after them. Billy's top team – George Wilson, T.W. Wilson, Cliff Barrows, Grady Wilson, George Beverly-Shea, Tedd Smith, Sterling Huston – they've been together forever. The advantage of this is that you become best friends and there are no egos or internal politics involved. They all just love each other as dear friends. There have been times when I've sat on a stage and watched Cliff Barrows watch Billy during a portion of the crusade, and I knew that Cliff knew exactly what Billy was thinking

at that moment. It was like they could read each other's minds without even having to talk about it. ... All of our senior leadership are 'lifers'. We've been together twenty-plus years and have committed to growing old together. Much of the growth at Saddleback can be attributed to this team of one mind, one spirit, identical values, close friendship, and personal commitment to each other for life.[1]

In many churches, in addition to the main leadership team there are other teams at work. Even in very small churches there can be teams, even though they may not be recognised as such: two people working together are a team. An entire church can be considered a team – which is a great opportunity for a small church.

In larger churches, non-vocational leaders – volunteer leaders – often carry larger responsibilities and at the same time have workplace responsibilities, and family and social commitments. One leader told me that it seems as though their senior lay leadership fit church in between social activities, sports events and family. Another leader said: 'Getting co-leaders to fulfil their commitments is a major issue for us. Some items remain on the agenda for months on end. The common response is something like, "I haven't had the time to do that yet."' How can we resolve this?

First, it may be necessary to understand how this kind of situation develops. Have we viewed leadership in terms of status and position rather than ministry? I have known Christians be eager to be appointed as a senior leader only to find they have little or no time to give to the position. Have we spent time explaining to potential new leaders what the commitments might be if they are appointed to the leadership team? In many churches the answer is no. You need to take into consideration the current commitments of potential leaders before appointing them.

---

[1] Harold Myra and Marshall Shelley, *The Leadership Secrets of Billy Graham*, Zondervan 2005, pp. 243–44.

The situation may be exacerbated by involving all the leaders in every decision. This means that the agenda is too full and too much time is taken up in holding meetings. One of the lessons for a leadership team in a larger church to learn is that not everybody has to know about everything. This calls for a change of thinking. Many church members expect all of their elders, deacons and parochial church council members to know all that is happening in the life of the church. Leaders do need to know whom they can refer to for answers, but they don't need to know the answers themselves.

In my experience we involved the entire leadership team only in issues that the entire team needed to be involved in. Otherwise leaders handled issues in the areas for which they were responsible, for example, worship, discipleship, pastoral care, etc.

Leaders need to be divided into small groups:

> The design department at Fiat is a small group. We don't have any committees, so there's no reason for us to take 24 to 36 months to develop a car. If a company is taking that long, it probably means communications are not working well, there are a lot of revisions going on, and you don't have the right team with the right vision.[2]

Then there are teams within teams. Paul Beasley-Murray, Senior Minister of Central Baptist Church, Chelmsford, writes:

> Our church is big on teams. The teams themselves are small in size and do not normally number more than seven members. The mandate of the team members is not to do all the work themselves, but to empower and encourage others in the church to get behind whatever may be their particular project.[3]

---

[2] Frank Stephenson, Chief Designer of Fiat as quoted on *BusinessWeek Online*, 16th January 2006.

[3] Paul Beasley-Murray, *Transform Your Church*, IVP 2005, pp. 164–65.

The following is an example of teams within a church. These are some of the teams at Frinton Free Church where I served as Senior Minister:

Catering Team	Weekday Crèche Team
Sound System Team	Audio-Visual Team
Reception Team for our	Ladies' Ministry Team
drop-in centre	Cleaning Team
Coffee Pot Team (our coffee shop)	Communion Preparation Team
Parents and Toddlers' Team	Youth Team
Bible Group Leaders' Team	Children's Team
(house groups)	Pastoral Carers' Team
Missionaries' Support Teams	Banner-Making Team
Sports Ministry Team	Alpha Group Team
Stewards' Team	Newcomers' Team
Prayer Teams	Maturity Matters Team
Finance Team	Mission Matters Team
Church Office Team	Ministry Matters Team
Bereavement Support Group Team	Information Table Team (Sundays)
Music and Worship Teams	Welcome Team
Art Workshop Team	
Flower Ministry Team	

What are the characteristics and principles that enable a team to function and cause it to be strategic? Once again, let us use a simple acrostic (based on the words TEAM SPIRIT) to help us remember some of the key points.

Transform lives

A strategic team works together to bring about transformation.

Jesus said, concerning people, 'I have come that they may have life, and have it to the full' (John 10:10). The New Testament is full of stories of lives transformed. The disciples were changed from fishermen to followers of Jesus Christ. Zacchaeus was changed from being dishonest to being honest (Luke 19:1–10); Saul of Tarsus, who fiercely persecuted Christians, became a Christian himself, and a leader as well, who planted churches and nurtured them.

The Oxford English Dictionary definition of the word 'transform' is to 'make change in the form' with reference to 'outward appearance, character, or disposition'.

The Bible puts it this way:

> Therefore, I urge you, brothers and sisters, in view of God's mercy, to offer your bodies as living sacrifices, holy and pleasing to God – this is your spiritual act of worship. Do not conform any longer to the pattern of this world, but be transformed by the renewing of your mind. Then you will be able to test and approve what God's will is – his good, pleasing and perfect will. (Romans 12:1–2)

An effective leadership team will seek ongoing transformation for themselves as well as for others. The kind of transformation that the New Testament speaks about is a life-long journey.

Transformation is the goal of strategic leadership. The church that stands still and refuses to change will die, even if it takes years to do it, because others keep propping it up!

In many churches there is an urgent need for a transformation of thinking – a radical change of mindset. Although in many parts of the world, particularly south of the equator, the Christian church is exploding with growth, this is not generally true in Western culture. In the UK, for example, the church has been in decline for most of the twentieth century, and the rate of decline has increased during the early years of the twenty-first century. For example, on Thursday 14th September 2006 the front-page headline of the *Western Mail* announced, 'Alarm as thousands more of us shun church in Wales'. Inside the newspaper a full page documented the decline. Barry Morgan, Archbishop of Wales, was reported as saying, 'People have faith, believe in God, but do not have much to do with the institutional church.' Average church attendance in Wales fell by 4 per cent in just one year. Over five years, from 2000 to 2005, attendance fell by 40,000.

There are, of course, places where the church is growing, but decline is the big news of the past hundred years. Other books and sources document in detail the decline. One sad observation on these reports is that churches seem more worried about the image of dwindling congregations and the inevitable resultant loss of funds, buildings and clergy than the fact that thousands of people are not benefiting from understanding and applying authentic biblical faith and values.

The main reason for decline is irrelevance. There are two ways in which many churches are, and were, irrelevant.

First, during the early years of the twentieth century great changes were taking place in British culture, and in the West generally. While these changes were taking place, the church, for the most part, stood still. During the second half of the nineteenth century churches grew considerably. Many were bursting at the seams. Consequently, new buildings were erected, seating thousands of people. The story of one church in the north of England can serve to illustrate what happened in thousands of others.[4] 'There are indications that church attendance was showing signs of declining in the first decade of the new century and this trend was certainly not helped by the disruption of the War in the second decade. Sunday school attendances had fallen drastically in 1920 compared with 40 years before.' From 1925 until 1934 'concern over decreasing congregations and the financial deficit steadily grew. It is true that there were occasions when the glories of bygone days were revived but only too fleetingly.' After the Second World War, 'the magnificent buildings erected in the previous century were now a burden on the diminished membership.'

---

[4] From my book *50 Ways to Help Your Church Grow*, Kingsway 2000, pp. 23–24.

Eventually, in 1955, this particular church agreed to sell the premises and find a new site. The new building was much smaller.

Such a story was repeated over and over again during the twentieth century in the UK. Although the congregations became smaller and were accommodated in newer and smaller buildings, what was happening inside those buildings was basically unchanged from the turn of the century. The church therefore lost its connection with the culture and became increasingly irrelevant to the changing world. Styles of worship, and in particular the language in which Christianity was expressed, changed very little. Although vocabulary changed, so that instead of speaking in the language of the Authorised Version, people began to preach in the language of the twentieth century, the church was still using language from the past. For example, as late as the 1990s a preacher in a televised worship service was describing the time when Jesus and the disciples were caught in a storm on Lake Galilee. The preacher was not using any long words, but his vocabulary was out of date. 'When the storm arose', he began. If a newsreader was reporting such a story, he or she would probably say something like, 'When the storm broke' or 'When the storm struck'. The preacher went on to say that the disciples 'cried to him in their distress and their cry went unheeded'. This is outdated language.

So even at the end of the twentieth century, many churches were still using a language and style of communication that were outdated. Added to this, many churches did not address the issues of the day.

Fifty-four percent of Jesus' reported teaching ministry rose out of the issues posed by others. He answered people's questions – spoken and unspoken. Peter's agenda in Acts 2 was not set by a lectionary . . . but by people's questions about the extraordinary behaviour they had just seen.[5]

---

[5] Mark Greene, *Supporting Christians at Work*, 'How-to Guide' vol. 2, no. 6, *Administry*, 2001, pp. 24–25, 72.

The second way in which the church is still irrelevant to most people is through its introversion. Too many churches are unknowingly too inward-looking. It has been said that the longer someone is a Christian, the less they think like a non-Christian. The expectation of many congregations is that the church is there to care for *them*. They want to worship in a style that suits *them*. Even the most apparently contemporary style of worship contains language and vocabulary that connect with Christians but not with the unchurched. The end result is an unspoken and sometimes unacknowledged attitude that 'church is for us' as Christians. A massive transformation takes place in a church whose worshippers realise they are not existing for their own benefit but are there for the benefit of the community. It has been said that the church is the only organisation that exists for the benefit of those who are not yet in it. Such sentiments have been expressed time and time again, but still the majority of congregations in Western culture worship and communicate in a way that suits them, rather than in a way that connects and communicates with the local community. So much of what happens in church on a typical Sunday is relevant only to those who have been Christians for some time. Christians won't bring non-Christians to church because the Christians are embarrassed. They know the worship will meet their needs as Christians, but they are not sure if it will meet the needs of their non-Christian friends and neighbours.

A strategic leadership will set about changing the mindset of the church from looking in to looking out, helping people to see that although the Christian community is a place where they can expect to grow and continue to change, part of that growth and transformation is to think outwardly and understand that the church's primary task is to go and make disciples. Much more will be said on the subject of relevance in a later chapter.

In the spring of 2006 I heard Rick Warren say that he wanted to bring about five changes:

1. I want to change the way unbelievers think about Jesus.
2. I want to change the way believers think about life and the church.
3. I want to change the way pastors think about preaching.
4. I want to change the way the church thinks about the world – not as the enemy, but as the mission field.
5. I want to change the way the world thinks about the church.

He went on to say:

> I want to restore credibility to the church.
> I want to restore responsibility to the believers.

The team that consistently seeks change and transformation for themselves and the churches they lead will have a unity of purpose that will strengthen the team.

Explore new ways of being a team

The strategic team needs intentionally to set aside some time to explore new ways of being a team and being a Christian community. To explore new ways may be the responsibility of just two or three people who have an interest in research. Some churches manage this kind of exploration very effectively, using just a small group of people.

The whole team does need to come together for a brief time on a regular basis. For example, one church tries to get every team member together every Wednesday for about one hour. That includes the pastor, the worship team, the children's team, the administration team – just about anybody who belongs to a team in that particular church. They have a meeting that contains the same parts each week:

○ *stories* – about God and about life-change. Every week they start with the question, 'Where have you seen God at work in or through the church in the past seven days?' This is a great way to spread the vision. It would be easy to forget why we do what we do (sweep floors, answer phones, prepare lessons, set up the drums) without the constant stories about changed lives.

○ *spotlight* – sometimes they spotlight a ministry in the church, letting the leaders of that area talk about what they do and their dreams for the future.

These weekly meetings keep them connected and keep the vision alive. They need not take place every week, but once every two weeks or once a month.

Accommodate each other's strengths and weaknesses

We have already said in Chapter 2 that we need to show each other grace. There is a need in a team to accommodate each other's strengths and weaknesses, to allow people to make mistakes and to recognise that mistakes will happen. We need to help each other learn from our weaknesses and from our mistakes. There is also a need to cultivate a culture of forgiveness.

Accommodating each other may include making allowances for one another, as members of the team may be passing through a learning period of life. Granting sabbaticals, leave of absence and time for recovery are all important for the health and welfare of the team.

Manage the church

Part of the team's role is management, particularly for the main leadership team. The word 'manage' is often rejected by Christian congregations. They associate it with the business world. They want to be 'pastored', not managed. Many are surprised to discover that the word 'manage' is used in the New Testament, and in particular with reference to leadership.

Here is a trustworthy saying: If anyone sets his heart on being an overseer he desires a noble task. He must manage his own family well and see that his children obey him with proper respect. (If anyone does not know how to manage his own family, how can he take care of God's church?) (1 Timothy 3:1, 4–5)

To pastor and care for the church means to manage the church. Pastoring and caring for one another does not happen automatically, though many think it should. Even in the New Testament church, caring and providing for others needed a degree of organisation. In Acts 6 the apostles exercised leadership by working out an arrangement whereby certain widows, who were being neglected, were provided for in the daily distribution of food (Acts 6:1–7).

Sometimes a distinction is made between a leader and a manager. Hopefully, the core leadership team will contain both. However, managers are leaders, and although leaders focus mainly on developing relationships, they too exercise a degree of management.

Sacrifice for the sake of others

A spirit of sacrifice characterises a healthy team. This is more than giving each other grace: it is taking a sacrificial approach towards ministry and leadership. Jesus said, 'If any of you wants to be my follower . . . you must put aside your selfish ambition, shoulder your cross, and follow me' (Mark 8:34 NLT). This refers not only to part of life but the whole of life. Frequently the process of denying oneself and taking up the cross is thought of in terms of repentance and faith, i.e. the process of becoming a Christian. But the principle continues after we have become Christians and are part of a Christian community. Some Christians willingly deny themselves so-called worldly pleasures in order to follow Christ but will not deny themselves spiritual pleasures in order to be all that Christ wants them to be. Not to have worship in the way that you would like it or prefer it for the sake of the newcomer is self-denial and taking up the cross. In a church where radical changes were taking place in order to reach the local community, an elderly deacon exclaimed to his pastor, 'I don't like it, but I'll do it, because I can see it is working.' That man was showing Christian maturity. After all the years he had been following Christ, he was still practising the principle of self-denial and cross-bearing.

Here is a vital life principle: '"Everything is permissible" – but not everything is beneficial. "Everything is permissible" – but not everything is constructive' (1 Corinthians 10:23).

There is a need for a deeper level of sacrifice among Christians today. All too easily decisions are made that fail to take into account the impact upon other Christians, other leaders and the church as a whole. If one leader of the team needs to be absent for part of the week or a weekend, it will help if another team member is not away at the same time. This requires that team members consult with one another before making such decisions. Balancing priorities is a complex process and one in which a measure of self-denial and sacrifice is involved. In his book *Courageous Leadership* Bill Hybels remembers when three advisors came to him on behalf of the church and said,

> The best gift you can give the people you lead here at Willow is a healthy, energised, fully surrendered, and focused self. And no-one can make that happen in your life except you. It's up to you to make the right choices so you can be at your best.[6]

---

[6] Quoted in Harold Myra and Marshall Shelley, *The Leadership Secrets of Billy Graham*, Zondervan 2005, pp. 265–166.

Self-management and -sacrifice are a priority if a team is to be healthy and effective. Without such commitment to Christ, no team will build a truly strategic church.

Pray together

'The team that prays together stays together' is, like any cliché, true. If the members of a team want to build healthy relationships with each other and exercise good leadership, they need to be intentional about finding time to pray together. Christ himself is our example. So many times he withdrew from the crowds and spent time with his Father in prayer. He also taught the disciples how to pray. There must have been times when they prayed together as a team.

Within any team there are going to be different temperaments. Some team members are going to be reflective and find it easy to stop and give time to prayer. Other team members will be activists. They get up in the morning and hit the ground running, and they find it difficult to slow down and give time for prayer.

Praying together must be a priority. Those who are good at it need to encourage those who find it more difficult. Not only as individual leaders and believers do we need to express our total dependence upon God, but also as a team we are totally dependent upon him. All effective and influential leadership teams have disciplined themselves to pray together. The dynamic spiritual power of a team comes from prayer. Members of a healthy team at any level in church life will spend time praying for each other and praying for those they lead.

Include, not exclude

A healthy team needs to work hard at making sure that every team member feels included. The larger the team, the more likely it is that someone within the team can feel as though they are on the outside. However, even in a team of three it is possible for two to be so close that the third member feels excluded. Each team member needs to feel that they are valued and appreciated, and that their ideas are listened to and given proper consideration.

It is very easy to let someone in a team slip away. It is normally a gradual process, and only when it reaches a certain point of separation does it appear that there is a crisis within the team. Team members need to be sensitive to one another's temperaments, strengths and weaknesses, and also to their points of view. Never let any issue become personal. If a team member seems to be out of step with the rest of the team, they cannot be expected to change without being appreciated, valued and loved. Be careful about confrontation. The Bible is clear that we should speak the truth in love (Ephesians 4:15), and in so doing we shall grow up and become more Christlike.

The Bible is very clear how we should behave towards one another. For example, 'Do not let any unwholesome talk come out of your mouths, but only what is helpful for building others up according to their needs, that it may benefit those who listen' (Ephesians 4:29).

Reward achievements

Christians are not always quick to recognise one another's achievements. In some circles it is regarded as unspiritual to give praise or thanks or to receive it. Many of Paul's letters begin by giving praise, thanks and appreciation to the leaders of the churches to whom he is writing. It is healthy to blend praise with expectations of learning and growth. People need to be encouraged, and a primary way to do that is through praise. There is nothing compromising about giving people more praise than they might deserve. A leader of integrity will not work for praise and reward, only the approval of God, but most people respond positively to a word of appreciation and encouragement from their peers.

In the parable of the talents Jesus comments that the master, having been pleased with his servant, says, 'Well done, good and faithful servant!' (Matthew 25:23). Jesus recognised the place of praise and reward.

A healthy team will also celebrate one another's accomplishments or the combined accomplishments of a team. Each step of learning or achievement or overcoming a problem can be a time to celebrate. One of the factors in some growing churches is that they have celebrated every step of health and growth.

In the church I led for 18 years we worked hard at making visitors welcome. To know whether or not we were achieving our objective we needed more than mere perception on the part of church members. Some churches think they are welcoming when in reality they are not. How did we know we were achieving our objective of being a welcoming church? We asked visitors to fill in a little card in which they stated what they first noticed when they came into the church. There came a point when 95 per cent of those cards said that what visitors first noticed was the welcome and the friendship. Because this response was consistent we knew we were reaching our objective. And so we thought it appropriate to celebrate. We not only celebrated as a team, but we shared this good news with the congregation as a whole. But there were a few who thought we were being unspiritual, drawing attention to ourselves, patting ourselves on the back and blowing our own trumpet. The majority, however, rejoiced that we had reached our common goal. We celebrated the fact and gave praise and thanks to God.

The power of encouragement, appreciation and praise is significant.

Invest in one another

Members of a healthy team will invest in one another's lives, and together, of course, the team invests in the total team of the church. Investing time and energy needs to be an intentional process.

Again, our supreme example is Christ himself, who invested much of his three years' ministry in the lives of the disciples. Without that investment we would not be here today as Christians.

One of the ways to start the process is by asking yourself, 'Who is it in the past who has invested in my life, and how have they done it?' We learn from those who invested in us so that we can invest in the lives of others.

Investing in the lives of others brings together many of the principles we have already spoken about – encouragement, prayer, learning opportunities, self-sacrifice, giving each other grace, speaking the truth in love, and much more.

Thank God for those who have influenced you the most, and ask him to help you influence the lives of others. Just as parents invest in children, so leaders invest in one another and the people whom they lead.

Translate ideas into words and pictures

Translating means taking time to help people understand why you are doing what you are doing. Communication with each other within the team, and the team communicating as a whole with the community, is of major importance. A leadership team will translate the vision they have to the church and the community as a whole.

Communication within the team is vital. There is nothing more disappointing and discouraging than a member hearing from someone outside the team what the leader or the team as a whole has decided. However, this issue is about more than just communication. It is translation. This is saying, 'This is why I believe what I believe' or 'This is why I am doing what I am doing.' It is translating what an idea means or what the implications of a particular vision are. It is about translating thoughts and ideas into reality so that people can understand and implement.

In closing this chapter, I want to acknowledge that, in my experience, leaders can't always choose their team-mates. However, you can raise the quality of your team, often despite difficult circumstances.

A good team spirit will include loyalty, respect, trust and a commitment to shared goals. Admit your own limitations. Remember that God uses ordinary people to do extraordinary things. Use humour. Learn to laugh at yourself. Have fun times as a team.

'Over time a good team works increasingly well together because they can anticipate one another's reactions and handle the inevitable surprises in a co-ordinated way.'[7]

Once a team intentionally includes commitment, trust, respect and an *ésprit de corps* based on a shared vision and sense of purpose, and is totally dependent upon God, expect change. Such teams can build strategic churches.

---

[7] Harold Myra and Marshall Shelley, *The Leadership Secrets of Billy Graham*, Zondervan 2005, p. 50.

4

Relational Structures

Let's recap what has so far been identified as going towards making a strategic church. It starts with a leader or leaders (Chapter 2) who are servant-hearted and think strategically. These are leaders who, among other things, depend entirely on God, who tell their story, who develop healthy relationships, who are obedient to the Great Commission, who nurture others, who are generous in spirit, who provide the lead that their church needs, who encourage, who admit their own limitations, who delegate, who equip others, who release others for ministry and mission, and who safeguard, harmonise, inspire and cast the vision. A strategic church is birthed by strategic leadership.

The next step is for leadership to become a shared responsibility (Chapter 3). Share the responsibility for transforming the church. Explore together new ways of being church. Accommodate one another's viewpoint. If you are the team leader, accept the responsibility for managing yourself, the team and the church. Have a sacrificial spirit. Pray together. Include each team member. Reward and affirm others in the team. Invest time and energy in one another, and continually translate the vision into pragmatic practice.

Now let us look at the actual structure of a strategic church. Everything has to have a structure; it's what kind of structure that makes the difference.

A strategic church builds on the foundation that the church is a family. Everything about the church flows from this biblical understanding of the church. Hebrews 2:11 (NLT) reminds us: 'So now Jesus and the ones he makes holy have the same Father. That is why Jesus is not ashamed to call them his brothers and sisters.' 1 Timothy 3:15 refers to 'God's household, which is the church of the living God'.

The emphasis therefore is on developing healthy relationships. As in any family, the church family needs to work hard at this. 'Make every effort to keep the unity of the Spirit,' says the Bible (Ephesians 4:3). Such unity is an 'effort' because God has made us all different, and the closer we get to each other, the more we see one another's distinctive ways and temperamental idiosyncrasies. As we know, it's easier to love some people from a distance than close up.

Most churches need to work harder at building healthy relationships, both within the church and with the local community. Strategic churches are a relational network rather than a Sunday morning institution.

Some churches are like a billiard table where the billiard balls crash into one another with unbelievable insensitivity and end up bouncing all over the place as a result of such collisions. Unless something is changed, the tragic result is deeper and deeper pain and anguish.

Outside the church many Christians are closed off to whole sections of the community, where people are divided into social classes, ethnic groups and religions. They look across the chasms of differences and subconsciously say to themselves, 'What do I have in common with those people? What do they have that might be of worth to me?' Some Christians made up their minds a long time ago about what certain kinds of people mean to them and have unconsciously structured their churches around certain limits. In more than one church I have personally heard individuals say, 'We don't want those kinds of people in our church.'

Structuring around healthy relationships means a radical change of mind-set in some churches. Some find that so hard to do, yet those same churches wonder why more people are not attracted to them.

In the tenth chapter of Acts we read about a specific milestone in the life of the early church. It is the story of how the church broke out of its natural boundaries and began to relate to people of other cultures. God used two very different people to bring about this change: Peter the disciple, and Cornelius, an officer in the Roman army. Two more different people it would be hard to find. From a human standpoint we might ask the question, 'What could these two men possibly have in common? What could Peter possibly mean to Cornelius, and what could Cornelius mean to Peter?' But God's vision is bigger than ours. God is wanting to unite for the benefit of all at the point at which we are we are so willing to divide and separate.

Getting ideas on how to welcome new people, how to organise small groups, how to lead a worship service, how to run a coffee shop or lunch club, how to set up a sports ministry is, in many instances, only tinkering around the edges of change. Until there is a fundamental change of outlook nothing significant is going to happen.

The health of relationships between leaders, and leaders and congregation, determines the path along which and the speed at which change can take place to bring the church to a strategic level. It has to be said that the health of relationships between the senior minister or leader and the rest of the leadership team is crucial. Far too many churches make no progress because of the poor relationship between the senior leader or leaders and the congregation. Personal preferences, a desire for power and control, competitiveness, jealousy and an unwillingness to see another person's point of view are all barriers to the church's health and growth. The sticking-point in many churches is the power struggles that take place in parochial church councils, elders' meetings, deacons' meetings or church meetings. Unless the infighting in a church can stop, it will never become a strategic church. So attention must be given to the kind of relationships that leaders have before considering the structure of the church.

Rick Warren puts it this way: 'Real change that affects the structure of your church begins with renewal, and any corporate and structural renewal begins with you.'

In order to change the structure, there must be renewal in your church. There are four kinds of renewal:

1 Personal renewal

Personal renewal comes when your heart warms up to Jesus Christ, and you become more aware of the presence of Christ and the filling of the Holy Spirit in your life.
Personal renewal always has to happen first. If you try to change your church without personal renewal in the hearts of the people, it isn't going to last.

2 Corporate renewal

Corporate renewal comes after personal renewal. You see it when the body of Christ begins to warm up. People begin to love each other and to make things right with one another. Restitution is made, sin is confessed, and barriers are broken down. There's warm fellowship in a church that's been corporately renewed.

3 Purpose renewal

The renewal of purpose (or mission) is when the church begins to realize, *we're here for more than just to have a good time and feel good. We have a mission, an objective, a purpose*. It's when people say, 'We're not here to have a little *Bless Me group*. We're here on mission and for a reason.'

The first two kinds of renewal – personal and corporate – occur quite often in many churches, but little comes from it because we don't get to the third and fourth level.

4 Structural renewal

When you have personal renewal and corporate renewal and purpose (*mission*) renewal, inevitably the church starts growing. But when it starts growing, you'll eventually need to make organizational changes because you can't put new wine into old wineskins. If you insist on keeping the old wineskin, it's going to stifle the growth.

Now, here's the catch: **You can't start with the fourth kind of renewal**. If you start trying to change your structure without having *personal, corporate* and *purpose* renewal, then you may get your head chopped off! People don't like to change unless their hearts have been warmed and prepared for change.

© Copyright 2000 Rick Warren

Strategic churches are characterised by structures that focus on being relational. Instead of organising around traditional departments, organise around strategic teams. Don't structure for control, but structure for ministry and mission. Let's look more closely at these *relational structures*.

Review the current structures

Some structures create division. They inadvertently foster competitiveness and status. In some churches, even in very small churches, structures are exceedingly complex. They are bureaucratic and, as a consequence, inhibiting. Key questions to ask are: Is your current structure actually serving the purposes of the church? Has the structure become an end in itself? Are people simply serving the structure? Are they spending so much time on meetings and committees that they have little time for ministry and mission, or even each other?

As you review your structures, think again about your vision and purpose. Remember that the work of the church is not called to fit the church's structure, but the structure is called to serve the church and enable effective ministry. Structures need to be viewed as support systems, a means to an end, rather than ends in themselves.

Eliminate the negative

Negative thinking and negative attitudes have been the bane of some churches, and although leaders often complain that their congregations have a negative attitude towards change, leaders themselves are sometimes setting the pace by their own negativity.

One of the obvious ways to avoid this is to focus on the positive. As the song says, 'Accentuate the positive, eliminate the negative.' The sequence is correct.

Negative thinkers attract negative followers. Positive thinkers attract positive followers. Focus on the good news. Focus on what is right in the church. A clear biblical example of this is to be found in Philippians 4:8: 'Finally, brothers and sisters, whatever is true, whatever is noble, whatever is right, whatever is pure, whatever is lovely, whatever is admirable – if anything is excellent or praiseworthy – think about such things' (NIV Incl.).

Eliminating the negative doesn't mean that we overlook the inevitable weaknesses of the church or what is obviously wrong in it. Leaders have a responsibility to face up to what is wrong, but they are more likely to do that if they are 'built up' a little at first. When we look at our strengths we are more motivated to deal with our weaknesses.

When the church in Ephesus receives their letter (Revelation 2:1–7) they are commended for what they have done right before they are told to correct what is wrong. However, even then, they are told to think positively and remember their 'first love'.

'Remember the height from which you have fallen! Repent and do the things you did at first'(Revelation 2:5), i.e. remember when you were strong, when you got things right. This is not to be mistaken for a call to return to past structures, but to remember the strength of the love and commitment that you are capable of, and to apply that love in the future. When we pray for renewal we do not pray for past glories but for new glories.

Listen to the viewpoint of others

Listen to the viewpoint of others on your team. Listen to the viewpoint of members of the congregation. Listen to the people who make up your community. It is sometimes implied that the Christian church is answering questions that nobody is asking. We need to listen to the questions that people are asking, both in the church and in the local community. Listening takes time and energy, and for some people it is actually quite hard work! Part of the process of building a relational structure is to listen to one another's point of view. The Bible says, 'clothe yourselves with compassion, kindness, humility, gentleness and patience' (Colossians 3:12).

Align church departments with church purposes

Align the departments of the church with the purposes of the church. The purposes of worship, fellowship, ministry, discipleship and mission need to be expressed in an overall sense of purpose for the whole church. This has to take into consideration the culture of the local community and the people that the church is trying to reach. The benefit of such alignment is that people are travelling in the same direction, sharing the same vision and 'working together with one heart and purpose' (Philippians 2:2 NLT). Alignment is a process and, as such, will take time, but it's never too soon to take the first step.

One way to begin is to align the Sunday or weekend sermons with the focus of small groups and personal daily devotionals. This is what happens in a journey such as 40 Days of Purpose or 40 Days of Community (part of the Purpose Driven Church movement, details of which can be found at the end of this book). These 40-day journeys reinforce the message on a daily and weekly basis. The kind of unity, purpose, focus and alignment that is produced is a rare experience for many churches. It takes time, but the process begins with an aligned and unified leadership team planning for the future.

I remember when two Bible college students spent five weeks intensely appraising the effectiveness of the work of our church. One of their conclusions was that every person they spoke to, from whatever department of church life they came, shared the same vision for the church as a whole. My response to that? 'At last we've made it!' However, having achieved such alignment and unity of purpose, it has to be sustained.

Transfer relational principles into the whole church

Transfer the foundational principles of a relational structure into all the ministries and activities of the church. All the principles that make up a healthy leadership team need to be transferred to the other teams in the church and into the church as a whole. A key component of healthy relational structures is, of course, small groups. 'Sadly, unless a church is prepared to structure its life around small groups, true fellowship will never really be possible.'[1]

Small groups enable relational structures. Someone who had resisted being part of a small group all his Christian life makes this point very clearly:

> In retirement I joined a small group at Frinton Free Church, which has a membership of about 600 people. Immediately I was made

---

[1] Paul Beasley-Murray, *Transform Your Church*, IVP 2005, p. 46.

welcome and played my part in the group, where I felt very much at home. The large church suddenly became very personal. I know that in reality nothing becomes significant or powerful until it becomes personal. There is a real depth of pastoral care. Together we find ways of serving the whole church and, through the church, the local community. Our small group really makes the whole church relevant to daily life. After 48 years I finally joined a small group and realised what I had been missing.

Many churches have made the 40 Days of Purpose journey as a means of encouraging people into small groups and building healthy relationships. One leader writes:

> We hoped it would build good relationships and it has. Over 90 percent of the church joined groups, and people who weren't in groups before now want to continue. It has opened many people's eyes to the reality that there is much more to church than Sunday.[2]

Structuring around small groups is key to a healthy and growing church. Some ministry teams may themselves be a small group. 'A ministry team is nothing more than a small group of people with a complementary assortment of gifts and abilities who are committed to a particular ministry that supports the ministry and mission of the church.'[3]

Influence: leadership is influence

Leadership is not about status or titles. Leadership is about influence. If you want to know whether you are a leader, ask yourself if there is someone you are influencing towards being a more wholesome person. Foundational to a pastor's leadership must be his or her ability to influence others in a positive way, but

---

[2] Mark Madavan in Mark Greene and Tracy Cotterell, *Let My People Grow*, LICC 2005, p. 8.

[3] James Emery White, *Rethinking the Church*, Baker Books 1997, p. 102.

this happens only in the context of relationships. Influence happens when you know your people and get alongside them.

Leadership, however, is not limited to leaders. Every Christian has the capacity to influence others either negatively or positively. Sadly, negative influence is not always recognised by the person asserting it. For example, a critical or destructive comment about the church overheard by an unchurched person or new believer can have a far-reaching negative outcome far beyond the realisation of the person who made the comment. We each have the responsibility to influence others positively and not negatively.

Strategic leaders influence others in the church with new ways of thinking and resist discouragement.

A legend is told of how God decided to reduce the weapons in the devil's armoury. Satan could choose only one 'fiery dart'. He chose the power of discouragement: 'If only I can persuade Christians to be thoroughly discouraged, they will make no further effort and I will be enthroned in their lives.' The exercise of encouragement within the small group ensures that the devil has no place.[4]

Observe where God is working

Whether or not you are a leader, observe what God is doing in people's lives. As an old hymn says, 'Count your blessings, name them one by one, and it will surprise you what the Lord has done.' If we take the time to look, it may surprise us what God is doing. As is so often said, we are followers. We need to see where the Holy Spirit is at work and follow him. Observe where Christ is working in the local community. And, of course, observe where he is working in the life of the church – not only your church, but other churches as well.

---

[4] *Ibid.*, p. 47.

Be ready to learn from other churches. Everyone knows that while there is no such thing as a perfect church, there is something to be learned from nearly every church. Sadly, some churches seem unwilling to learn from others. They feel threatened by the very thought. They feel they should be the originators of new ideas. That is the kind of pride that prevents churches from growing into healthy biblical communities.

Negotiate on non-essentials

Sadly, most congregations fall out with one another over secondary issues. When disagreements and different points of view emerge, learn to negotiate. Obviously, there are some matters that are non-negotiable. These will involve the gospel – the *kerygma*, the biblical principles and values you seek to live by and the truths you uphold. However, there are very many things in the life of a Christian community that are clearly negotiable. Strategic churches will often have a list of things that are non-negotiable, which have to do with their beliefs and their purpose, and which people coming into the church need to accept if they are to become members. Then there is another list of things that are negotiable, which usually have to do with buildings, styles of worship, denominational issues, different versions of the Bible, and the times and venues of meetings and activities, etc.

Negotiation calls for relational skills such as patience, a willingness to see another person's point of view and a genuine desire to try to understand where that person is coming from – and, of course, a readiness to explore what can be changed.

Affirm others

Whether or not you are a leader in the church, be intentional about affirming one another. If you are not a leader, then affirm your leaders. If you are a leader, affirm one another within the leadership team, within the other teams in the church and within the community as a whole.

Affirm newcomers as well as those who have been in the church a long time. In too many instances, newcomers have to earn affirmation over a long period. Affirm those who have a different point of view from yourself. Most of us like to be affirmed and valued for who we are and what we can do. Nothing brings out the best in people as much as this kind of affirmation. It helps to build self-esteem, and it reminds us that all of us have been affirmed by God. Jesus affirmed the disciples. God wants every person to know how much he loves them and that he has a purpose for them, and we want them to know that as well.

Love one another

Jesus said to the disciples, 'A new commandment I give you: Love one another. As I have loved you, so you must love one another. By this everyone will know that you are my disciples, if you love one another' (John 13:34–35 NIV Incl.). There is no doubt that people are attracted to a church where love for one another is incontestable. And when that love overflows into the community, it isn't long before that church is on the path to becoming a strategic church reaching out in love to the hurting people in the neighbourhood.

Summarise what your church is all about

Strategic churches are where people are regularly reminded of who they are and what their church is all about. Therefore, frequently summarise what the church is all about, its purpose and focus. Some churches use the first Sunday at the start of every year to remind the congregation of their purpose. This is sometimes expressed in the form of inviting people to enter into a covenant.

I always used the first five Sundays of the year to preach through the five purposes of the church: worship, fellowship, discipleship, ministry and mission. A summary of what the church is about can be expressed through slogans and symbols using carefully made banners, bookmarks, credit card-sized laminated cards, video clips and even songs, all to remind people of what it means to belong to their particular local church.

People today in the West lead very busy and full lives. Their attention span is short. With so many voices clamouring for attention via the media, the church is in competition to capture people's imagination and commitment. Therefore a constant reminder is necessary to keep people focused. Almost on a weekly basis you can summarise where the church is going and what its strategy and purpose are – something like, 'This is where we were last weekend, this is where we hope to be next weekend, this is where we are today.'

Trust and take risks

The kind of relational structure we are talking about involves trust, and trust always includes risk. Trying to run a church without making any mistakes is impossible. We can become so anxious to make sure everything is done properly that we slowly strangle the effectiveness of the church. Structuring for growth calls for the leadership to trust the membership and the membership to trust the leadership. How many churches are prepared for this level of trust? As a church grows, it becomes impossible for everyone to know everything that is going on. If, as a church member, you are prepared to trust your leaders, even when they make mistakes, provided they are genuinely seeking God's purposes, and if, as a leader, you are prepared to trust people with the ministry of your church, then you can move on to becoming a balanced, healthy, growing church.

Research, and never stop learning

Rick Warren frequently reminds leaders, 'The moment you stop learning, you stop leading.' Church leaders in particular should constantly engage in new research. We live in a changing world. Local communities change. Methods used by the Holy Spirit change. It is necessary therefore to take time out to do research. Main leadership teams should have the opportunity for sabbatical leave, during which time research can take place that is applicable or relevant to the leader's ministry, or to the church as a whole, or even to the wider church. It is also important to allow members of volunteer teams in the church to have breaks when they can refresh their thinking.

The way a church did something last year may not work this year, so there needs to be ongoing research into what works and what doesn't. Questions need to be asked, such as: Where are we succeeding and where are we failing? How is our community changing? What is it that people are now interested in? How do people view the family unit? This kind of research is always going to benefit a local church and enable it to be more strategic in reaching and serving the people within its community.

> For many people, Sundays may be days for doing other things than church, but according to a Church of England report 'Churchgoing Today', a growing number choose to attend weekday and evening services instead. The author, Revd. Lynda Barley, suggests that churches should offer 'alternative and attractive' services for people unable to go to Sunday services who may otherwise 'drift away' from regular church attendance altogether.[5]

In the UK an organisation called Christian Research has served churches well by making available the results of their research into various social and church trends in the nation, and providing

---

[5] *Daily Telegraph*, 7th July 2006.

some helpful figures and statistics. It was Christian Research that drew to national attention the dramatic fall in the numbers of youth and children involved in church over very recent years.

Employing the results of research keeps a church strategically connected to the community.

Underline key ministries and activities

Regularly underline and highlight the key ministries and activities of the church. This is another way of reminding people what the principles and values are by which, as a Christian community, we are called to live. Never be apologetic about reminding people of important issues. We have a strong biblical example of this. When Peter the disciple and apostle wrote his second letter he said,

> Dear friends, this is now my second letter to you. I have written both of them as reminders to stimulate you to wholesome thinking. I want you to recall the words spoken in the past by the holy prophets and the command given by our Lord and Saviour through your apostles. (2 Peter 3:1–3)

Earlier in his letter Peter also wrote: 'So I will always remind you of these things, even though you know them and are firmly established in the truth you now have. I think it is right to refresh your memory' (2 Peter 1:12–13); 'And I will make every effort to see that after my departure you will always be able to remember these things' (2 Peter 1:15). Jesus said to the disciples one day that the 'Holy Spirit, whom the Father will send in my name, will teach you all things and will remind you of everything I have said to you' (John 14:26).

So we need not be defensive or apologetic when we remind people of important issues by way of underlining those issues and regularly drawing them to their attention.

Clarify your vision

Regularly clarify your vision for the church. Whether or not a church will be strategic depends on the leaders' ability to clarify their vision and to lead the process of change. If the pastor or leader is not deeply convinced about the direction in which the church should go, then the vision will fade. Vital to leading change and implementing vision in a local church are the clarity and conviction in which the leader understands and communicates God's heart for the future of the church. Sometimes this is best done in the context of a church residential weekend or an away-day. This is the time when people can disconnect from the everyday business of the church to allow the Holy Spirit to clarify future direction and anchor that vision in the minds and hearts of the people.

Train to develop gifts

There is a balance between allowing people to exercise their gifts in ministry and helping them to grow and develop. Opportunities need to be provided whereby people can receive help and training to develop their gifts and use them more effectively. Volunteers need time and opportunity to be trained as much as those working for the church full time. Encourage people to take the time to be trained. This may mean encouraging them to use their spare time or even part of their holiday to receive training. If people are truly captivated by the vision of the church and are growing in their commitment to Christ and their desire to live by his purposes, they are more likely to invest their time and energy into training. Sadly, all too often people in churches are appointed to tasks for which they receive no training, or they are not willing to give the time to be trained.

Upgrade to give God the best

This may be a surprise to some, but it's another way of reminding ourselves that the church needs to update and upgrade its equipment, its standard of teaching and training, and the materials and tools that it uses. Continually upgrade the quality of your communication. Upgrade the quality of your pastoral care. You can upgrade the quality of your worship. We want to offer the very best that we have and are to God for him to use. In times past churches have often opted for second best, and it has proved counter-productive in terms of mission and outreach.

Neglected buildings, old office equipment, poorly produced literature, cluttered platforms and rooms and untidy, out-of-date noticeboards do not help a church to be strategic!

When I was a teenager there used to be a church in Worthing's High Street that was strong and lively. I don't know why the building was sold or the circumstances behind the fact that a congregation no longer worships there. However, two or three years ago I discovered it is now a pub and night club. It is called 'The Church'. The name is written in neon lights. Because the building is listed, the new owners have had to retain the pulpit (from which a disc jockey now functions), the organ loft and the baptistery, which has a fountain in the middle. The exterior of the church is also carefully preserved. One Sunday evening, as I looked through the now wide entrance, 'The Church' was crowded with youth in a way it never was before. These were youth who go regularly to 'The Church'. I couldn't help thinking how warm and inviting, bright and attractive it looked. And I thought, 'Perhaps if the church had upgraded the building to be more bright and attractive and welcoming, it might still be the church.' Of course, the church is far more than a building, but the building is a tool, and the principle of upgrading applies to material tools.

Respect one another

Respect is another value that lies at the heart of a relational structure. We not only listen to one another and learn from one another, affirm one another, love one another and trust one another, but we also have respect for one another. There will be times when you will be called to respect the choices and decisions that other people make, even if you do not agree with them. Lack of respect has probably been at the heart of many divisions in church life. People are more likely to deal with opposition to their ideas or different points of view if they know that they are still respected. Respect also has the capacity to draw the best out of people.

Within the various teams in the church and within the small groups and in all the relational structures, respect for one another needs to be uppermost. Never allow differences of opinion to become personal and, as a result, cause misunderstanding and division.

Evaluate ministries

Tom Patterson, a well-known and highly regarded strategic process thinker, in his book, *Living The Life You Were Meant to Live*, designed an assessment grid called the 'Four Helpful Lists Matrix'. These 'four helpful lists' are built on four poignant questions that will help you evaluate any of your ministries or events. For each ministry and event he suggests four questions:

1. What went right? Optimise that.
2. What went wrong? Change that.
3. What was confused? Clarify that.
4. What was missing? Add that.

A tool like this encourages participation from team members, and maybe the congregation too, capturing the collective thinking and reflection of the church. Optimise what is right; change what is wrong; clarify what is confused; and add what is missing.

Support one another

Leaders of strategic churches understand the importance of support for one another and support for every member of the church. The word 'support' sums up most of what we have been talking about in this chapter. People will not function efficiently if they do not feel supported. On the other hand, the higher the level of support, the more confident people will be, the more they will learn from their mistakes and the more enthusiastic they will be to grow and learn.

And now a final word on relational structures.

Many churches manage to think through and write out a purpose statement expressing why they exist. Some churches will go a step further and write out a vision statement expressing where they want their church to be in two, five or ten years' time. Not so many churches go on to the third statement, a mission statement, describing how they intend fulfilling their vision. The process looks like this:

• a Purpose Statement – why we exist
• a Vision Statement – the future we strive for
• a Mission Statement – how we will accomplish the vision

It is the 'how' factor that makes a church strategic. Not too many churches get to this point in their thinking. This is the area of hard work. For example, at a recent leaders' conference the question was asked, 'Our existing vision has been in place for ten years. It now seems dated. How can we build on it?' Not only does the vision need reviewing, but clearly the church hasn't moved from the vision statement to the mission statement. If you wait too long before implementing the vision, it will die.

Questions to ponder

How is your church creating opportunities for people to build relationships with one another?

How can you make being a part of your church family more meaningful?

How can you become more purposeful in your relational structures and in how you achieve the purposes for your local church?

How can you ensure that members of your church feel loved and cared for?

What does God expect from the members of your church?

What can newcomers expect from your church?

What are the plans for incorporating new people into your church?

What are some of the ways in which you can be sensitive to the needs of the unbeliever?

How whole-life is your church? (See the questionnaire in Appendix 1.)

5

Application Preaching

A major step towards making a church strategic and closing the so-called sacred–secular divide is to change the preaching. Recently the Methodists in the UK have had the courage to say that a lot of their preaching is dull. 'A major survey of Methodist ministers in the UK reveals they have an overwhelmingly negative opinion of Methodist worship and preaching.'[1] There were many reasons given for this, such as 'The majority of Methodist ministers feel they give too little time to study, routine pastoral visiting, and to preparations of sermons and worship – due to the competing demands on their time.'[2]

I was recently asked the question, 'How do we prepare relevant preaching series with a wide range of folk in the average Sunday congregation, which stretches from those who have been Christians for a very few weeks to those who have been believers and been well versed in the Bible for over 50 years?'

My experience is that the unchurched and believers can be served in the same message, because both are looking for practical truth by which to guide their lives. Applying the Bible to our everyday lives rather than preaching it as a history book can communicate to believers and unbelievers. This is not dumbing

---

[1] John Buckeridge, *Christianity Magazine*, September 2006, p. 9.

[2] *Ibid.*

down or compromising the message. Rather, the reverse is true. The more I apply the Bible in a practical way, the more congregations comment that this is deeper teaching, including those who have long been used to a more conceptual or Bible-study style of preaching. When unchurched people are going to be present in a weekend worship service, any wise preacher considers their struggles and asks God how to apply his word to their lives as well as serving the more mature disciples.

The majority of churches on most Sundays of the year are preaching to themselves. The average Sunday message is for those who have at least some background knowledge of the Bible. It is hard to break out of that mould. Most clergy and preaching teams are trained to prepare their messages with mature Christians in mind. And over long years we have educated congregations to expect this and think of the weekend messages as being for them.

It takes a great deal of time and creativity to present biblical truths in ways that Christians and non-Christians will understand. The solution is application preaching.

> I think one of the biggest problems in Christian education is the unstated goal of helping people grow in knowledge. Since we are trying to teach the truth, we feed folks lots of facts. But the bigger goal should be to help people grow in faith. That means appealing not just to intellect, but also to imagination.[3]

People of faith and of no faith cope with many of the same issues in life. There is a common humanity that embraces us all. Generally speaking, people want to know how best to manage relationships, how to overcome their problems, how to cope in the workplace and, above all, how to make sense of living in today's fast-paced, rapidly changing, hurting world. Remember, this is true for mature Christians as well as new believers and non-believers.

---

[3] Steven James, *Recapture the Mystery*, Revell 2006, quoted on webpage for Rick Warren's Tool Box, issue 271, August 2006.

You will discover, if you haven't already done so, that they will positively respond to this approach to preaching.

The gospel addresses all of life's situations. We need to have that basic conviction. Human nature has not changed. Help people to grasp how practical the Bible's teaching is. We have good news to share. We want to identify with Jesus when he quoted from Isaiah (Luke 4:18–19):

> The Spirit of the Lord is on me,
> because he has anointed me
> to preach good news to the poor.
> He has sent me to proclaim freedom for the prisoners
> and recovery of sight for the blind,
> to release the oppressed,
> to proclaim the year of the Lord's favour.

'Jesus came . . . preaching' (Mark 1:14 AV). Proclaiming the good news is a priority for churches that are trying to be strategic. Jesus went to Galilee to preach God's good news. 'At last the time has come!' he announced. 'The Kingdom of God is near! Turn from your sins and believe this Good News' (Mark 1:14–15 NLT). Preaching the good news has a vital role in strategic churches. It is the number-one task that the church is called to do. The apostle Paul told the church of the Thessalonians, 'The Lord's message rang out from you' (1Thessalonians 1:8). That's a strategic church.

'The apostles were teaching the people and proclaiming in Jesus the resurrection of the dead' (Acts 4:2). That verse is talking about the disciples Peter and John, who later said, 'For we cannot help speaking about what we have seen and heard' (Acts 4:20). Jesus said, 'the Father who sent me commanded me what to say and how to say it' (John 12:49).

The Christian church has many tasks, including of course: modelling a lifestyle; being Christ to the community; and living by the principles of righteousness, mercy, justice and peace. However, the foremost task of the church is to proclaim the good news. The Bible says of the apostles, 'they never stopped teaching and proclaiming the good news that Jesus is the Christ' (Acts 5:42).

Strategic churches recognise the supremacy of proclaiming the good news. It can of course be proclaimed in a number of different ways, even by what we might refer to as the 'silent witness'. 'Always be prepared to give an answer to everyone who asks you to give the reason for the hope that you have. But do this with gentleness and respect' (1 Peter 3:15).

Various pieces of research have shown that the number-one reason why so many people are leaving the church is lack of relevance – lack of relevance in terms of the content of the message and the presentation of the message, for even where the content may be relevant it is often hard to understand because of poor presentation.

According to Bishop Tom Frame, even today's top theologians have been told that they 'have a duty to make their work accessible'. He goes on to say, 'While their works are rightly acclaimed, they do not give up their meaning easily.' His fear is 'that people will simply give up reading theology'.[4] It seems to be that right across the board, at least in Western culture, Christian speakers have difficulty in presenting and applying the Christian message in a relevant way. In contrast, preachers who have the ability to present profound truth in ways that ordinary people can understand are those that have gathered the crowds.

Gaining and holding the attention of people is not easy. It never has been. Sadly, however, it has not, and still is not, always seen as important. In the nineteenth century, the great preacher C. H. Spurgeon addressed his students on the subject, saying,

> Our subject is one which I find scarcely ever noticed in any books upon homiletics – a very curious fact, for it is a most important matter,

[4] Tom Frame, *Church Times*, 2nd June 2006, p. 10. Dr Tom Frame is the Anglican Bishop to the Australian Defence Force.

and worthy of more than one chapter. That overlooked topic is, How to Obtain and Retain the Attention of our Hearers. Their attention must be gained, or nothing can be done with them: and it must be retained, or we may go on word-spinning, but no good will come of it. They must be awake, understanding what we are saying, and feeling its force, or else we may as well go to sleep too.[5]

One church leader commented that in today's culture 'attendance at Sunday services is fitted in between social activities, school events and family commitments'. This is a common statement by clergy who get frustrated that fewer people attend a whole series of teaching messages. How can we disciple people if they do not attend? We have to accept that in the twenty-first century people, even much older people, are more mobile and families are more scattered than they used to be. Also, school and sports activities seem to draw people away. Research indicates that more people are going to church less often.

We can be frustrated about this or we can accept it and work with it in a number of different ways. One way is to offer CDs and transcripts of weekend messages and encourage members of the congregation to keep 'up to speed'. In my experience, they will try. Another way is to make the message so compelling and relevant that they do not want to miss it.

Spurgeon had much to say about preaching that is practical and still applicable to the twenty-first century, such as being aware of people's backgrounds, circumstances and situations. In his day he would reprimand the student who preached so long that the farmer in his congregation was late milking the cows. Apparently the farmer said of the student, 'How would he have liked it if he had been a cow?' Spurgeon talked about the importance of varying the voice continually. Don't indulge in monotones.

---

[5] C. H. Spurgeon, *Lectures to My Students*, 1st series, Marshall Brothers Ltd (date unknown), p. 136.

'Vary your speed as well. Vary the tone. Human nature craves for variety, and God grants it in nature, providence and grace; let us have it in sermons also.'[6]

Don't lose sight of the purpose of preaching, which is to develop Christ-like convictions, Christ-like character and Christ-like conduct. This is what it means to go and make disciples. Because preaching the good news is so vital to making disciples, we all struggle with it. It is my personal conviction that the devil uses every tactic he can to discourage, degrade and distort God's chosen method of proclaiming salvation, namely preaching. Let us look at some practical ways forward in application preaching.

Address the issues

A lot of preaching takes place Sunday by Sunday without any reference to what is going on in the world, the church, the community or people's lives. Whenever I start to prepare a sermon I always ask myself a number of questions: Who is likely to be in the congregation? What is likely to be on people's minds at this particular time? Where is this particular church in its journey? What is happening in the local community? And what is happening in the wider world? This approach to preparing a sermon is criticised in some circles as a sell-out to consumerism and lack of faithfulness to Scripture. I would argue the exact opposite. If we follow the example of Jesus, we shall find that the majority of his preaching arose out of issues and questions posed by others. Peter Brooks, a respected BBC religious broadcaster, said over 20 years ago, 'We need to speak to their felt needs in such a way as to reach through them to deeper needs than ever they have been aware of.'[7]

---

[6] *Ibid.*, p. 142.

[7] Peter Brooks, *Communicating Conviction*, Epworth Press 1983, p. 11.

This principle can apply to systematic expositional preaching, only in this instance issues will come up as they appear in the particular Bible passage being dealt with. There is much merit in this, as it means that certain biblical passages are not overlooked. However, this approach can result in preachers neglecting to address the needs right in front of them and at the time when they come along. The best way is to have a balance of both topical and expositional preaching. Application applies to both.

Pray over every message

It is important to pray about every message that we proclaim. Just as Jesus said, 'For I did not speak of my own accord but the Father who sent me commanded me what to say and how to say it,' (John 12:48–50) so Christian preachers need to be as sure as they can be that what they are saying is coming from God, and that how they are presenting the message is also coming from him. Spend time in prayer asking the question, 'What does God want me to say this morning?' Wherever I am preaching, in my own church or visiting another, having asked the questions about what is happening in the world, the local church and the community, I then ask the question, 'What is it that God wants me specifically to say?' It is amazing to me that when God gives us the message, he also gathers the people he wants to hear it. The Holy Spirit prompts people to attend church when there is a message that he wants them to hear. The alternative is that the Holy Spirit does not prompt people to attend church where there is a message that is irrelevant and that has been prepared without any real consultation with God, whose representative we are supposed to be.

This approach requires time spent in prayer – considerable prayer. Prayer is just as much part of preparing the message as the practicality of choosing and interpreting Scripture, addressing topics, and thinking about human hurts and needs. While preaching a series of messages on the different issues that people face in everyday life, I once felt compelled to preach a sermon on the dangers of alcoholism. Part of the way through the sermon I had planned for a recovering alcoholic to share her story. When the service was over I was amazed to discover that there were six people in the congregation who did not normally come to church and who were struggling with alcoholism. We were able to offer specific help. I am convinced that people turn up when we speak what God wants them to hear. This only comes about through spending time in prayer.

Prepare thoroughly and in plenty of time

Don't leave it too late to prepare. With so many pressures on ministers, preparation has sometimes been left until the last minute. Spend time thinking about the Scripture reference, the topic and how best to present the message. Personally I spend an average of 6 hours to prepare a 25–30-minute sermon. If the sermon was to be shorter, 10 or 12 minutes in length, then it would take more than 6 hours to prepare. I begin the first stages of my preparation at the latest on Tuesday. It will not be fully formed until Friday. If you are using PowerPoint, then the main structure of the message illustrated with it needs to be completed by Thursday. This is assuming that you preach one message a week. Obviously, preaching both morning and evening, i.e. two sermons, is going to take up approximately 12 hours. The benefit of working with a team is that there is more than one person who can preach.

There are many books on preaching and how to prepare a Sunday sermon, but I strongly recommend the 'Preaching for Life Change' course taught by Rick Warren. More than anything else, this has changed the way preachers preach. He uses a method called C.R.A.F.T. This stands for:

C = Collect and categorise
R = Research and reflect
A = Apply and arrange
F = Fashion and flavour
T = Trim, tie and title

(For more information on this course, please see Appendix 2.)

Try not to rush preparation. Think seriously about the message over and over again. Howard Hendricks says, 'The higher the predictability, the lower the communication'. This means that we need to work hard to surprise people. When people know what's coming, they're not paying attention. For example, television commercials are always deconstructing where you think they're going, and they interrupt the flow in order to get your attention. They cause us to ask such questions as, 'What is this all about?' 'What is this supposed to be advertising?' By the time the product concerned appears on the screen, the advertisement has already got our attention. In the majority of sermons most people know exactly what's going to happen, which is why they don't come to church. Deconstruct not just for shock value but for improved communication, so that you can better make the point you are trying to make. You have to make sure your message gets through to people. They are bombarded with many other messages during the week. An advertising executive speaking on BBC1 said that in the UK people receive an average of 33,000 messages a week.

Learn everything about the subject

Soak yourself in the message so that if necessary you could preach it having left the notes behind in a desk drawer. Let the message occupy your heart and mind so that it becomes a part of you.

You can never learn too much about the message. Aim for excellence in the content as well as the presentation. But don't feel you have to use all the material and information you have gathered. Learn as much as you can and use what is relevant to your congregation, perhaps leaving them with just one or two practical principles to apply.

Introduce the purpose of your message

Too many congregations go out of church on a Sunday saying, 'It was a good message, but I'm not sure what he or she was trying to say.' It is sometimes helpful right at the very beginning of a worship service to introduce the purpose of the message or the theme of the entire worship service, so that from the very beginning the congregation knows exactly where the service is going.

At the beginning of the sermon it is helpful to say something like, 'This is what we're going to talk about this morning', 'This is the issue that we're going to address' or 'This is how the Bible teaches us to deal with a particular need.' Introducing the purpose of the message at the beginning of the service or at the beginning of the sermon is much more likely to capture people's attention than waiting until part-way through or even until the end of it. This does not contradict the above point about deconstruction. Deconstruction takes place in the presentation.

Sometimes preachers will tease a congregation by using fancy titles, leaving them to guess what the purpose of the message is. That only works if you do finally reveal the import of your message clearly.

Clarify what you want to say

A helpful thing to do is to try to sum up the message for yourself in a single sentence. If a preacher cannot do that, it is a likely sign that it will not be clear to the listeners. If I cannot sum up a sermon in a single sentence, then I know that it is not going to be clear to the congregation, because as yet it is not clear to me.

Summing up the sermon in a single sentence clarifies the message and often shortens it, because as a preacher you realise more clearly what it is you are trying to say.

It is good practice to sum up the message in a title – more about that later.

Aim for relevance

The issue of relevance comes up again and again. This is because it is a big issue in nearly every church. As already stated, lack of relevance is the number-one reason why so many people no longer attend church. I cannot emphasise enough the importance of relevance. The fact is most preachers, including myself, believe that they are relevant, and, like the people in their congregations, they think the charge of irrelevance is meant for someone else. But it is clear that we are not addressing the issue of relevance enough, because every week thousands of sermons are preached and yet very little is changing. We need to think long and hard about this issue and spend much more time working on it.

In most instances it calls for preachers to adopt a simpler vocabulary and a simpler approach to preaching. Relevance is about teaching profound truth in simple ways. Too many preachers are frightened about being simple. They do not want to be thought of as lacking in depth. Also, it is much harder to present profound truth in simple ways. It takes time to break down the vocabulary and even the sentences and phrases so that everybody can understand what is being said. Don't confuse being simple with being simplistic.

Trim unnecessary material

Edit out unnecessary material. Take out all the unnecessary words. If you can say something in seven words, don't use twenty.

Trim the number of Bible verses you were going to use, because probably you have studied many more verses by way of preparation. Trim the background material. Your church members aren't nearly as fascinated by archaeology and linguistics as you are. Preaching is not a Bible lecture or a history lesson. Preaching is for life change. You don't have to explain everything about a text to your congregation. When we pay too much attention to secondary issues we miss the point and purpose of the message. People today do not want more information: they want meaning.

Trim your points. The Puritan preachers would sometimes preach 30 to 50 points, but exhaustive sermons are exhausting to the congregation. So trim the number of points. Most people can only remember three to five. Trim your quotations and illustrations. One of the most common mistakes is to spend too much time telling a story.

One of the advantages of writing a full manuscript is to be able to read it through and take out every sentence that is unnecessary or repetitive. This sharpens the message. It helps to make every sentence meaningful and helps the whole process of communication.

Illustrate for impact

Strike a balance in your use of illustrations. Some sermons have far too many stories and illustrations, and some have none at all. Obviously, a sermon needs some illustrations and stories. Very often these can be used as tension-breakers. Use illustrations and stories that are close to home. Make a break in the sermon by having another person tell their story, or, if you have the technology, use an appropriate video clip. Sometimes the only way to make a point is to wrap it up in a story.

Watch your language. Jesus said, 'the Father who sent me commanded me what to say and how to say it' (John 12:49). As

we move further into the twenty-first century, language is changing at an incredible speed. That's why there are so many new and
updated translations and paraphrases of the Bible. Louis Rosen-
feld and Peter Morville, in *Information Architecture for the World
Wide Web*, remind us that language is ambiguous and that words
can be interpreted in more than one way. Take, for example, the
word 'pitch'. There are more than 15 definitions of the word,
among them: a throw, a fling or a toss; a black, sticky substance
used for water-proofing; the movement of a ship in rough seas; a
presentation by a salesman; and the sound produced by the fre-
quency of vibration. Pay particular attention to new 'in' words,
but avoid the temptation to sound 'cool': it usually backfires!

Organise the presentation

You may have prepared well, but many a sermon falls down
through poor presentation. Such things as faulty public address
systems can limit the presentation of the message. The first few
words of a sermon are crucially important in order to grab attention. If those words are not heard, then the introduction to the
purpose will be lost, and it takes a while for both preacher and
congregation to recover from a faulty start with the sound system.
Obviously it is helpful to have sound checks before the worship
begins. Organise any video clips that may be used. Again, make
sure that the technical equipment is working properly and that
the person operating it knows exactly when to use the DVD or
any other kind of technical insert.

All too often I have been to churches where operators of technical equipment have said something like, 'Well, I'll see if it works
when we come to it. I hope it does.' Sometimes I haven't even
known which part of the platform I'm going to speak from. The
end result can be a preacher standing up on a part of the platform
that he or she has never been on before, using a sound system

that has never been checked, and not knowing whether the PowerPoint presentation or the DVD is in fact going to work. Lack of proper organisation for the presentation of the message weakens the confidence of the preacher and distracts the congregation.

Name the sermon

This is not quite the same as introducing the purpose of the message or saying the message to yourself in a single sentence. Nevertheless, the title ought to sum up the message. It should serve to remind both preacher and congregation of what the message is about. It helps if it is also memorable. I have actually had people say to me, 'Do you remember when you spoke about, or preached on. . .' and then they have said the title of the message. The title helps people to remember the message and easily refer to it. I have known people remind me of a message I preached as far back as 20 or 30 years ago, simply because they still recall the title.

Some sermon titles simply make no sense and do not encourage people to come to church. The following are examples of some that I have collected over the years, and I have wondered what they mean, particularly to the unchurched. Many of these titles assume a certain amount of Christian knowledge:

- Rediscovering the Radicalism of the Early Church
- God is Faithful
- Man's Extremity, God's Opportunity
- Playing Second Fiddle
- Don't Go There
- Either He Is or He Isn't
- The Darkness Gave Way
- Ten Ways to Guarantee Unhappiness
- Walking the Hard Road
- Where Is the Far Country?

- Only God Knows and He Refuses to Tell
- Concerning the Collection
- The Rupture of a Relationship
- Blurred Vision
- From Shadow to Reality
- The Garments of the Ungodly
- It Happened Out in the Country

Compare those titles with the following, for which I have included the relevant Bible references:

- How God Builds Character – 2 Peter 1:3–11
- How to Stay Calm in a Crisis – Joel 1:1–20
- Balancing Life's Demands – Mark 12:28–34
- How to Enjoy the People in Your Life – Philippians 1:1–11
- Coping with Change – Genesis 46:25–26
- The Secret of Being Content – Philippians 4:10–20
- How to Connect with People – Romans 12:1–8
- What to Do When Life Crashes in on You – Job 2:1–13
- How to Handle Life's Hurts – Job 3:1–26
- The Secret of Healthy Relationships – Philippians 2:1–11
- How to Resolve Conflict – Luke 22:24–26
- Handling Anger in the Home – Proverbs 29:1–27 and Ephesians 4:26
- What Would Jesus Do with My Money? – Matthew 6:19–34
- Facing the Future without Fear – Psalm 23:6
- How God Turns Evil into Good – Genesis 50:25–26
- How to Tell God that You Love Him – Matthew 22:34–40
- What Difference Does Forgiveness Make? Matthew 6:7–14
- How to Find Peace – Mark 3:20–35
- What to Do When You're at Your Wit's End – Psalm 107
- How to Make Wise Decisions – Proverbs 2:1–15
- Why Does God Allow Evil? – Matthew 13:24–30
- How Can I Handle Discouragement? – Nehemiah 4:1–15

- How Can I Ever Change? – Genesis 32:22–32
- Why Is This Happening to Me? – Genesis 50:15–21
- Why You Need a Church Family – 1 Peter 2:4–12

Preach a positive message

Some preachers seem to emphasise what the Bible is against rather than the hope it embraces. The gospel offers hope, purpose, direction, fulfilment, peace, something worth living for, principles and values to live by, acceptance and affirmation. The fundamental message of the Bible is one of hope. When Jesus stood up in the synagogue in Nazareth and announced his mission, he made positive statements. He quoted from the prophet Isaiah: 'good news to the poor'; 'freedom for the prisoners'; 'recovery of sight for the blind'; 'to release the oppressed'; 'to proclaim the year of the Lord's favour' (Luke 4:18–19). The gospel is essentially good news. Even repentance can be preached in a positive way: turning from darkness to light; from blindness to sight; from being lost to being found; from death to life.

Preaching a positive message does not compromise the truth. As Jesus did, we can preach repentance in a positive way without ever compromising the truth.

Represent the truth

This must always be at the forefront of our thinking. We are in no way to compromise the message. This doesn't mean that we return to long sentences and difficult words. Rather, it means that while we recognise that the methods of proclamation and preaching will constantly change, the content of the message will never change. Its interpretation and presentation will vary, but the fundamental message of good news will never change, even though it is expressed in different ways. Our hope lies in Christ, who died for our sins and rose again, overcoming death; and all who believe in him, the Bible says, will have eternal life.

Whatever form or shape the new expressions of church will take in the future, the gospel does not change.

Expect results

Having prayerfully prepared the message, we can look to God to act through the proclamation of his word. The story is told of how, many years ago, one of Spurgeon's students complained that people were not being changed through his preaching. Spurgeon responded by saying something to the effect of, 'Of course you don't expect people to become Christians every time you preach, do you?' To which the student replied, 'Of course not.' Spurgeon's response was, 'That's why it's not happening.'

We know that it is the Holy Spirit who ultimately convinces people of the truth, but Jesus gave us the clear command that we are to 'make disciples', and we are part of the process of people coming to faith in Christ. Of course, ultimately it is God's work, and because of that we can look to God expectantly, particularly if we have prepared as best we know how and have prayed that God will use the message he has given us to make himself real to people in the congregation.

Apply the message

Lack of application is where the vast majority of preaching fails. Much of my own preaching across the years could be summed up in three words: 'Be more committed.' But I never spent enough time telling people how.

Lack of application is a major problem in the church today. One of the reasons why some preachers do not make application of their message is because they've never been taught how to do it. They've read many books on interpretation but perhaps haven't ever read a single book on application, partly because there are not very many in print.

After every message is prepared I would recommend we ask ourselves the questions, 'How are we going to help people apply this message? What specifics can I offer people so as to put the message into practice?' Think of anything up to half-a-dozen ways in which you can help people apply the message. Often an inspiring message is lost in a relatively short time because subconsciously people are asking the question, 'Yes, but how?' YBH: these three letters are good to write in your sermon preparation notes after every major point.

Most of the preaching of Jesus was application, not least the Sermon on the Mount. Many of Paul's letters to the churches were also application. Don't preach just for the purpose of doctrine: preach for the purpose of change.

> All Scripture is inspired by God and is useful to teach us what is true and to make us realise what is wrong in our lives. It straightens us out and teaches us to do what is right. It is God's way of preparing us in every way, fully equipped for every good thing God wants us to do.
> (2 Timothy 3:16–17 NLT)

The great evangelist D. L. Moody once said, 'The Bible is not given to increase our knowledge. It was given to change our lives.' Over the years I've noticed that a lot of established Christians are interested in Bible knowledge – which is great. For example, a lot of Christians are interested in how Paul dealt with those who differed from him and wanted all the gentile Christians to be circumcised and obey all the laws and traditions of the Jews. Having heard about this, we can easily go out of church thinking we have grown. We haven't, unless what we have heard has changed our own attitudes, behaviour and understanding of how God wants us to live. All we will have done is gained more Bible knowledge.

Do you know that Bible knowledge alone is dangerous? Look

at 1 Corinthians 8:1 (NIV), 'Knowledge puffs up, but love builds up'; or 1 Corinthians 8:1 (NLT), 'Knowledge may make us feel important.'

Until you and I do something about what we have heard, none of us has really grown or made any progress spiritually. Unfortunately, a lot of preachers and Bible teachers have fallen into the same trap. They think that if they preach about how Paul handled those who opposed him, the people in front of them are growing.

Spiritual growth and discipleship are intentional on the part of the individual believer and must be intentional on the part of the teacher.

Give specific action steps. We could hear a sermon on how to be a better father and we might write, 'Yes, but how?' Or we could hear a message inviting us to study the Bible and we might say, 'Yes, but how?' We could hear an inspiring message on how to let the Holy Spirit control our life and we might ask, 'Yes, but how?' People say 'Christ is the answer', and most of the time they know, but they need to know just how he is the answer. Rick Warren has an application acrostic in which he suggests that after you have prepared your message you ask whether there is:

Attitude to adjust
Promise to claim
Priority to change
Lesson to learn
Issue to resolve
Command to obey
Activity to avoid or stop
Truth to believe
Idol to tear down
Offence to forgive
New direction to take
Sin to confess

These are twelve questions to ask when we look into the Bible and try to make a personal application to our own life.

Connect with your congregation

It is vital to establish rapport with your congregation. This is one of the purposes of the introduction. It was noticeable that Billy Graham spent several minutes at the beginning of each message establishing rapport with the people. Identify with the congregation, know who they are and where they're coming from. You have to establish a relationship before you can establish a response, so the first two or three minutes of your preaching are very important. You need to gain attention. In those first few minutes people are either going to tune in or tune out. Right at the beginning of our proclamation we need to answer the congregation's question: 'Why should I listen to this?'

A good introduction has brevity. At this point in the proclamation don't waste precious minutes. Don't start the same way every week. Sometimes start with a quotation, sometimes with a question, sometimes with a shocking statement and sometimes with a humorous story. One very important principle is not to subject the congregation to your particular mood. Never begin a sermon with an apology such as 'I'm not feeling too good today.'

Humour has its place

Humour is another tension-breaker. Don't overuse it, and don't use humour for the sake of it, but humour certainly has its place in preaching. Sometimes people are critical of humour: 'We're not here to be entertained.' This is a frequent comment from Christians who have a more sombre view of worship. The message is not to entertain in the way that a television programme sets out to entertain. However, there is an entertainment factor in preaching. The definition of 'entertain' is 'to capture and hold someone's

attention for an extended period of time'. That is what preaching
is all about. The crowds listened to Jesus with delight. A question
to ask, having completed your sermon preparation, is, 'Is there a
more interesting way to say this?' 'When God's word is taught in
an uninteresting way people don't just think that the pastor is
boring, they think God is boring!'[8]

Remember the lecture given by Spurgeon to his students,
quoted at the beginning of this chapter.

Invite a response

Having applied the message and provided people with specific
actions to follow up, we need to go one step further and invite a
specific response. If you have preached the gospel, offer an opportunity for people to receive Christ. Show them exactly how they
can do this, perhaps by coming to talk with you or someone else
after the service is over; or ask them to fill in a communication
card that they can hand in at the close of the service; or use the
come-forward invitation that evangelists have used over the
years. Clearly explain to people why you want them to respond
and how you want them to respond. Too many invitations are
misunderstood, and unchurched people have no idea what is
going on. Make the invitation clear. Take people through a step-
by-step procedure. Whatever the content or subject of the sermon, make it clear how people can respond, what they can do
about it and how they can apply it. Tell them the first step to take.

Notice reactions

As you come towards the end of preaching the message, try to
sense people's reactions. Simply looking at people's faces will help
you to understand whether their interest has been stirred or

---

[8] Rick Warren, *The Purpose Driven Church*, Zondervan 1995, p. 231.

whether they're longing to rush out of the door. Their reactions to your message will determine how you conclude and what kind of invitation to respond you will give. Some preachers conclude their message in ways that are inappropriate to the mood of the congregation. Responses are sometimes called for that are out of place, embarrassing and insensitive to the congregation's frame of mind at that moment.

Generate follow-up

Not only is it important to give specifics to help people apply the message and, if appropriate, to invite a response, it is also important to offer some kind of follow-up, again depending on what has been preached. For example, a sermon on 'how to manage your anger' could be followed up by offering further reading material or the opportunity to join a small group that is going to deal specifically with that subject. A sermon on 'how to get more from your Bible' may offer Bible study material to help people get started, or again an opportunity to join a specific group that offers further help. Another example would be 'how to manage your finances', and again further reading material or a specialised small group or counselling could be offered. Sermons on the subject of parenting can be followed up with parenting groups and classes. It is important that such follow-up is readily available at the close of the sermon.

Application preaching usually means a change of mind-set.

- In what ways could you improve your message preparation and presentation in order to effect life change?
- How sensitive are you to the presence of seekers in your worship service?
- In what ways might you be sounding patronising to seekers and new believers?
- List some ways in which you can make your preaching more compelling.

6

Training and Equipping

I receive more questions on this subject than any other area of church life. For example:

- 'What motivates people to serve Christ in the church, and in particular to engage in leadership?'
- 'I feel I don't have enough time to train new leaders, but if I don't, then I will become the bottleneck for what God wants to do, and I will burn out before too long.'
- 'How can we train and equip the leaders of tomorrow?'
- 'How can we disciple new Christians in their early twenties who have no background, as previous generations had, to deal with issues of sexuality, finance, commitment to worship etc.?'
- 'How do we help people feel they belong quickly, particularly if they are unbelievers or carry extensive personal baggage?'
- 'What comes after Alpha?'

In the course of this chapter, I hope these typical questions will be answered.

It is crystal-clear in the New Testament that the local church is to become a vibrant, ministering body on the basis of the gifts of the Spirit. This is what it takes to develop a fully functioning body of Christ that ministers effectively in the community and the world. These gifts are not to be confused with natural abilities.

The 'gifts' come solely from the Holy Spirit. They are supernatural endowments and are the result of God's work in the inner life of the believer. The distinction, however, between natural talents and gifts should not be pressed too far, because the gifts may very well blend with natural talents in the service of Christ. The list of the gifts of the Spirit makes it clear that they cover the entire work of the ministry of the church. Even then, the biblical list is probably not meant to be exhaustive. John Stott said in an unpublished lecture at Spurgeon's College, London, that there are probably 'thousands of gifts':

> Every age, culture, generation, and situation has its specific needs. Surely, the Spirit will step in to meet those needs by 'gifting' his people to meet them. At any rate the idea of the gifts of the Spirit makes it clear that God has provided in full measure for all the needs of the church in its growth, worship, and ministry.[1]

This view of the gifts of the Spirit means, as we have said, that churches should be structured around people. In other words, the church should start with gifted people and not programmes. The traditional way of structuring a church through councils and committees often ends up with the wrong person in the wrong job. The result is that both the person and the job suffer until next year's committee can appoint a new person – only to have the same problems all over again.

Strategic churches structure themselves on the 'gift' principle. Once the church takes this principle to its logical conclusion, it may say, 'If we do not have the people who are gifted to meet the needs of a particular ministry, then we drop that ministry.' This is the difference between a gift-led church and a need-driven church. Some small churches tend to be need-driven simply because they do not feel they have all the people necessary to do the work of the church. The more strategic view of the church is,

---

[1] Lewis A. Drummond, *The Word of the Cross*, Broadman Press 1992, p. 309.

then, revolutionary for many, and particularly the smaller churches for whom structuring around people will require a big step of faith. The revolutionary impact of this way of working is that the church becomes people-focused rather than minister-focused or need-focused. There is also a new awareness that all God's people are ministers and that everyone has a part to play in the life of the church.

Having recognised that God equips the church through the giving of gifts, it must also be recognised that the gifts need to be developed and nurtured. 'As the patron of gifts, the church must provide an abundance of unthreatening situations in which [believers] have an opportunity to consider for themselves all manner of adventures.'[2] One particular church takes this very seriously. As part of its morning worship the opportunity is given for anyone to stand up and, as they put it, 'sound a call'. This involves an individual saying, 'I have become concerned about this or that problem in our community, and I am searching for ways to help. Is there anybody else who feels drawn to this same thing? If so, meet with me and let us begin to explore what we can do.' People are 'called out' by certain concerns in the community. This is an authentic expression of what it means to be the church. The church is the place where we discover that God loves us individually, but that he loves the whole world as well. Church is where it becomes clear that God is very fond of us, but it is also the place where we learn that he is just as fond of everyone else as well. A strategic church is one where its members are 'called out' by concerns in the community and the world and then equipped by the Holy Spirit to meet those concerns in company with others who share them. It is in this way that the church becomes what God intends it to be – his gift to the world.

---

[2] Elizabeth O'Connor, *Eighth Day of Creation: Gifts and Creativity*, Word Books 1971, p. 47.

Strategic churches therefore focus on the gift development, training and equipping of their people, not to support the church as an institution, but to be part of a relational network of Christians who serve one another and the local community. This is a very different approach from those occasions when I have heard leaders only challenge their congregations to go out into the world. They say it almost with a sense of frustration. The response from the congregation may be an enthusiastic yes, but nothing actually happens. Why? Because the majority of Christians are already out in the world! The problem is they are not sure what to do out there, perhaps in the workplace, at the leisure centre or in the community as a whole. Some are self-taught, but many need help to serve in mission and ministry. If the average Christian knows 10 other people, then a church of 50 members is in a relationship with 500 people. 'The key to mission is to equip Christians for where they are, not where they are not; for where they have relationships, not where they don't.'[3]

Strategic churches discover people's giftedness and find ways to help them use their gifts and then support them in their developing ministries. Every church needs an intentional process by which to identify, mobilise and support the ministries of its members. In too many churches the whole process stops at the stage of just identifying a gift or ministry. So let us look at some practical steps to take.

Track new arrivals

Some churches fail to keep track of new people. It is not always that the new people are not welcomed, but they are not integrated into the life and work of the church. It is considered that

---

[3] Mark Greene, *Imagine*, London Institute for Contemporary Christianity 2003, p. 15.

they have to be in church a number of years before they can be trusted with a responsibility. In the meantime some new arrivals become early departures. 'We need to be creating an atmosphere of unparalleled welcome and acceptance in our places of worship.'[4] Some churches do not realise how many newcomers they get because they don't recognise them and have no strategy for keeping them. One church leader remarked to me that they didn't know how many visitors they had until they set up a welcome team.

The top three factors that draw people to church are:

1. the warm welcome they receive
2. the various activities of the church
3. the relevance of the teaching

The warm welcome is more than just a handshake at the door. It is a newcomer strategy: newcomers' meals; welcome packs explaining what the church is all about; and newcomers' small groups, where newcomers can meet each other as well as existing members and leaders of the church.

New people need to be tracked from the moment they step inside the building. At this point they will be subconsciously asking themselves such questions as, 'Do I fit in here?', 'Does anyone want to know me?', 'Is there anybody else here like me?'

Many churches believe they are welcoming, but that belief can only be tested by a visitor. I have stood in church halls drinking coffee after a morning worship service and the whole place is buzzing with conversation. For a moment it looks as though everyone is friendly and welcoming, and they are, but only to themselves. They are so busy talking to each other they simply fail to notice visitors among them. Helping people to feel quickly that they belong has to be an intentional process, part of the strategy.

---

[4] Sally Morgenthaler, *Worship Evangelism*, Zondervan 1995, p. 85.

Tracking new arrivals means having a strategy for welcoming them, incorporating them and before too long equipping them. People, particularly new people, like to be involved. There are exceptions to that, of course – if someone new arrives who has been very heavily involved in their previous church, they will probably look on this as an opportunity for a period of rest before being given a particular role in the life of the new church. However, my experience has been that new arrivals, particularly new believers, are some of the most enthusiastic and visionary people in your church. We often use them on the welcome team because although they may not know everything about the church they are the most enthusiastic welcomers of new people.

Remind people of God's purpose

Always keep the vision of ministry before your people. Communicate the importance of their ministries. When you recruit to ministry, always emphasize the eternal significance of ministering in Jesus' name. Never use guilt to pressure or motivate people for ministry. It is vision that motivates; guilt and pressure only discourage people. Help people see that there's no greater cause than the Kingdom of God.[5]

Remind people that God has a purpose for their life. This sense of purpose is what motivates people to serve Christ. I never believed that anyone joined our church by accident. I believe God brought every person into our church family for a specific purpose. The best strategy for reminding people that God has a purpose for their life is to make that truth a recurring theme in your preaching and in the small groups of your church.

I am convinced that part of God's purpose for his people is that they belong to his family. That finds expression by joining a local

---

[5] Rick Warren, *The Purpose Driven Church*, Zondervan 1995, p. 391.

church. In the busy days in which we live, there are those of course who say they have no time to get involved in the local church. Some of them have heavy work-loads which require working long hours. Consequently there is little time for the family and for leisure. I remember leading a local church conference when a number of men expressed frustration at the long hours they worked, the responsibilities they carried and then the constant reminder that they could be more involved in the local church. It was all too much for them to cope with.

There are two issues here. The first is that God's purpose for their life will include their role in the workplace and their responsibility as a family member, perhaps a parent. I knew of at least one man who between Sundays would travel many thousands of miles in holding down a particularly responsible job as a senior executive of a well-known international insurance company. The usual question put to him on a Sunday morning by fellow church members was, 'Where have you been to this week? Was it New York or Hong Kong?' This particular man said to me one day that he looked to his church to give him something to live for and something to live from. And he regarded his experience of worshipping with God's people at least once a week as a source of strength and inspiration for the busy week ahead. He was convinced that he was fulfilling God's purpose for this life.

However, there are others whom I would question whether their furious activity is part of God's purpose for them. These are the folk who have got themselves into a situation where circumstances have overtaken them. They work very long hours and carry heavy responsibilities because they have to earn the salary to keep them in the lifestyle that they have now become used to. I once challenged a group of men who were frustrated about not being more involved in the ministry and mission of the church by asking the question, 'Are you sure that this furious activity, where you are hardly at home and see little of your children, is really

God's purpose for your life?' Most of them admitted that they had never even thought about that question. They had always assumed that God's purpose for their life was confined to what they did in church.

Over the years I have seen some men and women, challenged by this question, actually change their lifestyle. They realise that this is not how God intended them to live. As a consequence they have downsized their home; in some instances taken massive cuts in salary; and then found immense fulfilment in discovering God's purpose for them in a less demanding job which enabled them to have more time with their family and more time for ministry and mission. Some have become vocationally involved in the wider ministry and mission of the church. There is nothing so life-changing as accepting the invitation of Jesus to 'put aside your selfish ambition; shoulder your cross; and follow me' (Mark 8:34 NLT). This is a long way from those who are somehow able to live a comfortable lifestyle and turn up on a Sunday morning and just enjoy a worship service that suits their particular needs.

Assimilate new people

Don't just welcome people and remind them that God has a purpose for them, but have a strategy of assimilation. This will help them to know whether or not yours is the church to which they could belong. An assimilation strategy can be quite simple. Not only do 'we need to be creating an atmosphere of unparalleled welcome and acceptance in our places of worship',[6] but we also need politely to ensure that we have a contact address and telephone number. Every few weeks at my own church we would invite newcomers to a newcomers' tea. There we would inform them about our newcomers' small group which met in my home.

---

[6] *Ibid.*

The strategy was that within a relatively short period of time new people were in the senior minister's home where they were meeting other new people and were learning something about the ethos and philosophy of our particular church. There was no pressure to join the church but rather an eight-week opportunity in which to consider whether or not this was the church that they would fit into.

From this newcomers' small group they would be introduced to other relevant small groups, depending on their Christian journey. Some would join a seekers' group, such as Alpha; others would join a group to discover more about their spiritual gifting and how they could be used in the life of the church and beyond; and others would join a spiritual growth group so as to discover ways in which they could grow in their new relationship with God and with their fellow Christians.

Our strategy was to provide folk with a track on which they could travel as they became part of the church family, grew as Christians, and were equipped for service in the church and mission in the world.

Imagine the possibilities

Imagine the church where far above the normal numbers of members are involved in its work and witness.

> I believe the church is a sleeping giant. Each Sunday church pews are filled with members who are doing nothing with their faith except 'keeping' it. The greatest need in evangelical churches is a release of members for ministry.[7]

Releasing members into ministry is the most effective way to disciple people. People learn in a variety of ways, but most learn best by serving in a ministry. Many discipling courses are based on

---

[7] Rick Warren, *The Purpose Driven Life*, Zondervan 2002, p. 365.

imparting knowledge. Knowledge is important, but change is what discipling is about. 'Moving members into ministry should be an ongoing process. Your placement process should focus on empowering people, not on filling positions.'[8]

Imagine Christians of all ages who are growing and developing in their faith, and are becoming what Mark Greene (of the London Institute of Contemporary Christianity) calls 'whole-life disciples'. This is a strategy that calls not only for a change of thinking on the part of leaders but also on the part of members to see themselves on a life-long spiritual journey rather than sitting in church for separate, individual, isolated experiences of worship week by week or month by month, or even less frequently.

Notify about ministries

Tell new people about the ministries of the church. In very many churches even longer-standing members have little or no idea of the ministries of the church. They are unaware of everything that the church is involved in, or what it does in the local community. Even in small churches I have heard people exclaim, 'I had no idea our church was doing that' or 'I didn't know our church was involved in this.'

Part of the assimilation, training and equipping strategy is to tell people about the various ministries of the church and what is involved in them, however small they may be. Most churches are surprised when they realise how many ministries they have. One of the features in the 40 Days of Purpose journey is to hold a Ministry Fair, a kind of Ideal Home Exhibition showing the various ministries in the church. On the occasion that we held our Ministry Fair people were overwhelmed to find over 40 different ministries on show, ranging from flower-arranging and cleaning

---

[8] *Ibid.*, pp. 381–82.

through to a weekly soup run for the homeless. Each ministry hosted a table displaying what that particular ministry involved. The big surprise of the day was 70 new people volunteering for the various ministries of the church. Notifying people about the tasks that the church is involved in and helping them to understand more about those ministries, what is involved and why we do them, helps people to decide whether to volunteer or not. Many folk in church are frightened to volunteer because they do not know what they're volunteering for.

Impress importance of involvement

Impress on members of the church the importance of getting involved in God's work. That may mean balancing time and energy between the workplace, the church and the home. In that mixture of responsibilities there needs to be a sense of direction and purpose – 'This is what God is calling me to do.' Some may come to an awareness, not previously recognised, that their work is their ministry and God's purpose for their life. People's commitments to the ministry and mission of the church will inevitably vary according to where they are in life and what other responsibilities they carry. But whoever we are, God calls each of us to live for his purposes. To all of us is given the biblical instruction, 'Be very careful, then, how you live – not as unwise but as wise, making the most of every opportunity' (Ephesians 5: 15–16).

> Invest time in teaching your members the biblical basis for lay ministry. Then teach it in classes, sermons, seminars, home Bible studies, and any other way you can emphasize it. In fact, you should never stop teaching on the importance of every Christian having a ministry.[9]

---

[9] *Ibid.*

Name the tasks

Name the tasks involved in the various ministries of the church. A lot of people are working in local churches by default. In other words, they have a feeling that no one else is available, and somehow they volunteered and have been stuck with it ever since. This does not send out a positive signal to encourage others to get involved in the work of the church.

Part of the strategy of training and equipping should be not only to answer the question, 'What kind of training and equipping do we need and how shall we do it?' but also 'Why are we doing it?' It is helpful to take the time to write out some job descriptions. Perhaps someone can do this who has a flair for this sort of thing or is not involved in other tasks. They would be prepared to interview others about what they do. Make these job descriptions available to new people so that they know what is involved. Writing job descriptions may also lead to the discovery that some people are doing some things unnecessarily.

The following is an example of how ministry tasks in the church can be classified and how people can be given some idea of what is involved and how long it takes. The example comes from the Saddleback Community Church.

- **Servant Opportunities** – Anytime, anything, anywhere
  - Time requirement: 1–2 hours a week
  - Gifts unknown and untested
  - Skills for specific task/experience helpful
  - General passion to meet a need
  - Seeker/new or young believer
  - Church membership not required

- **Stay-at-Home Opportunities** – Virtual and Ministry-in-a-Box

- ○ Time requirement: 1–2 hours a week
- ○ Skills for specific task/experience very helpful
- ○ General passion to meet a need
- ○ Church membership required

- **Seasonal Opportunities** – Easter, Christmas, Events
  - ○ Time requirement: minimal
  - ○ No experience required
  - ○ Unsure of gifts
  - ○ Spiritual maturity – seeker
  - ○ Church membership not required
  - ○ Willingness to serve where needed

- **Short-Term Opportunities** – Project-based
  - ○ Time requirement: 1–4 weeks
  - ○ No experience required
  - ○ Skills for specific task/experience helpful
  - ○ Church membership required
  - ○ Willingness to serve where needed

- **Small Group Friendly Opportunities** – Community Care, Easter, Christmas, Events, etc.
  - ○ Time requirement: various
  - ○ Willingness to serve where needed

- **S.H.A.P.E.-Based Opportunities** – Specific S.H.A.P.E.-focused opportunities within existing ministries
  - ○ Time requirement: 2–4 hours a week
  - ○ Gifts are starting to be developed
  - ○ Passion for ministry
  - ○ Some experience required
  - ○ Stable spiritual growth
  - ○ 101–301 S.H.A.P.E. completed
  - ○ S.H.A.P.E. Discovery Session completed

- **Servant Leader Opportunities** – Leadership positions in groups and ministries (small group leaders, ministry leaders, etc.)
  - Time requirement: 4+ hours a week
  - Proven gifts and people skills
  - Strong passion/ministry vision
  - Solid spiritual foundation
  - Leadership training completed
  - 101–401 S.H.A.P.E. completed

Give guidance

Don't let people volunteer under false pretences. They need to know as much as possible about what is involved in a particular ministry. This is why naming the tasks and providing job descriptions are helpful in deciding whether or not to volunteer.

Also, are they suited to that responsibility? Talk about other responsibilities they currently have, to see if the time is right for them to serve. They may need time to grow spiritually or to heal emotionally. Are they ready to serve? Are they already serving? Do they want to begin a new ministry? What are their gifts? Guidance can be given one on one or, better still, in the context of small group training or an equipping course such as the one described below.

Establish a gift discovery and training course/group

Put in place some kind of gift discovery and training course. If people shy away from the word 'course', think of it as a small group. We developed this kind of small group on a regular basis and used the S.H.A.P.E. syllabus, which a number of other churches have found very beneficial. S stands for spiritual gifts; H stands for heart; A stands for abilities; P stands for personality; and E stands for life experiences.

The S.H.A.P.E. model was developed by the Saddleback Community Church many years ago to explain the five elements that determine a person's ministry. Each one of us is shaped by God, and exploring these five aspects of development helps each member to understand their S.H.A.P.E. – how God has put them together so that he can use them to serve him by serving others. 'You will be most effective and fulfilled in ministry when you use your spiritual gifts and abilities in the area of your heart's desire in a way that best expresses your personality and experiences.'[10]

The S.H.A.P.E. material is taught in many churches and has proved to be an impressive method of attracting people into ministry. It is a significant part of training and equipping. (More details are included in Appendix 3.)

Qualify people

Everybody likes a little recognition. Nobody likes to be taken for granted. To give some people a level of qualification encourages them to continue learning. It helps them to know that they are delegated to carry a particular responsibility. The qualification may be as simple as giving some kind of recognition that a person has passed through a period of training and equipping such as the S.H.A.P.E. group. To give someone a title as a means of qualifying them is sometimes a mixed blessing. Sometimes it is necessary and helpful for both the individual and the church, but at other times it can become a burden and an embarrassment, and in some cases even go to a person's head! However, part of the strategy of training and equipping must be to recognise that a person has been identified, called and set apart for a particular purpose. This is the logical outcome of recognising that the gifts of the Holy Spirit are given for ministry. Above all, value your people. Spend

---

[10] Rick Warren, *The Purpose Driven Church*, Zondervan 1995, p. 375.

time with them. Affirm them. Listen to them. Update them. Keep them informed. Equip them and pastor them.

Unlock the potential

This is what Jesus did with the disciples, and it is what God loves to do with all of us. 'For this reason I remind you to fan into flame the gift of God, which is in you' (2 Timothy 1:6). 'Do not neglect your gift, which was given you' (1 Timothy 4:14). A strategic church will develop a strategy for helping people to fulfil their potential.

Remember, your placement process should focus on empowering people.

Here is a suggested set of 'ten commandments' on how to help people use their gifts:

1. Thou shalt not be too rigid or restrictive as to the nature of the gifts.
2. Thou shalt not wait to minister until you discover you're fit.
3. Thou shalt not get too subjective or existential.
4. Thou shalt not forget godliness and holiness in a disciplined life.
5. Thou shalt not forget thy responsibility to the body, the whole church.
6. Thou shalt not forget thy leader's role.
7. Thou shalt not forget the power of the Holy Spirit.
8. Thou shalt not forget others.
9. Thou shalt not forget the church and its need for revival.
10. Thou shalt not forget to witness and share Christ with the lost.[11]

---

[11] Lewis A. Drummond, *The Word of the Cross*, Broadman 1992, pp. 313–14.

Identify gifting

This is a specific section of the S.H.A.P.E. group, but whether you use that material or not, it is important that gifting is identified not only by the individuals themselves but by others around them. Sadly, some people believe they have gifts that in reality they do not have. And in other situations people have gifts that they have not yet identified and recognised but that others clearly have. 'The identifying of gifts brings to the fore another large issue in our lives – the issue of commitment. Somehow if I name my gift and it is confirmed, I cannot "hang loose" in the same way.'[12]

Identifying your gift is only part of the process of discovering someone's ministry. As mentioned above, other factors are identified in the S.H.A.P.E. course that determine a person's ministry.

Pursue excellence

Churches are notorious for settling for second best or doing things in a second-rate way. In such churches the members can quickly develop an attitude of carelessness. People end up not taking their responsibilities in the church as seriously as they take their responsibilities elsewhere. They will turn up at the last minute and be ill-prepared for whatever the task involves. People can get used to this way of working.

There really is no excuse for poor-quality material and poor workmanship simply because of carelessness or half-hearted commitment. Why should we offer God or people less than the best? There is a book called *100 Ways to Get Your Church Noticed* (see Bibliography). It calls attention to all kinds of ideas that will enable you to pursue a strategy of excellence.

---

[12] Elizabeth O'Connor, *Eighth Day of Creation: Gifts and Creativity*, Word Books 1971, p. 25.

Prioritise purpose

Some churches have no sense of purpose or direction, while other churches are trying to do too many things at once. Often there is a conflict in people's minds and strong competition for their time, because there are too many things happening in the church, and everybody thinks that their ministry is the most important. Where a church does not recognise its purpose, everyone else in the church will follow a purpose that they think is right in their own eyes.

No one church can do everything. No one church is good at everything. Work out and think through what God's purpose for your church is, and you will more quickly recognise the people he has sent to you to fulfil that purpose. Sometimes people are not engaged in the work of the church because the church has never recognised its purpose or the fact that certain people are sitting there whom God has sent to enable the church to fulfil its God-given purpose.

Having a sense of purpose both on the part of the church and the individual reduces frustration, eliminates conflict and competition, and creates an altogether better environment for everyone.

Inspire confidence

This may need to be done at several levels. Perhaps someone has just taken on a responsibility in the church for which they have not yet developed the necessary skills or gained sufficient experience, and they need to have their confidence strengthened. Others may have been working at a particular ministry for many years but have a problem with low self-esteem, and again their confidence needs to be encouraged. Throughout this whole strategy of training and equipping, from the moment a person gets on the track to the point where they are very much on the journey, people need to be inspired that they are doing God's work in God's way for God's glory. There can be no greater privilege or sense of fulfilment than knowing that you are part of what God is doing in the world today.

Note people's progress

Having equipped and trained people it is important to follow through, to note how people develop and grow and gain experience. As already mentioned, at times they need to be encouraged and maybe even rewarded in some way, perhaps by celebration or recognition of achievement. It is difficult to inspire confidence, to pursue excellence and to unlock the potential of a person without taking time to monitor their progress and development.

Galvanise commitment

As every serious Christian and strategic church has noticed, nothing happens without commitment. Throughout this chapter we have emphasised on a number of occasions the need for commitment. As implied earlier, there may be a reluctance on the part of some Christians to identify their gift because it means they will have to make a stronger commitment to the body of Christ, in the context of which the gifts are to be used. The Bible is clear that the gifts are not to be used in isolation outside the body of Christ. The Bible is indeed transparently clear about that: 'Now to each one the manifestation of the Spirit is given for the common good' (1 Corinthians 12:7). The New Living Translation puts it this way: 'A spiritual gift is given to each of us as a means of helping the entire church.'

Commitment may seem to be in short supply these days, but most people are committed to something. The issue is about prioritising our commitments. God makes it clear that he wants to be the first in our lives. In the Old Testament we find this wonderful promise: 'For the eyes of the LORD range throughout the earth to strengthen those whose hearts are fully committed to him' (2 Chronicles 16:9). Oh, to be such a person and to encourage others to be the same! The promise in that verse of scripture is that God will strengthen those who choose to be fully committed to him.

In order to galvanise commitment it is helpful to put together a statement that expresses a commitment that people can be invited to share in. An example of this kind of commitment is found in the Purpose Driven Covenant that the members of the Saddleback Community Church were invited to enter into on the occasion of the 25th anniversary of the church. (See Appendix 4.)

An intentional strategy to help people to be strategic will build a strategic church.

7

Exponential Thinking

Strategic churches think exponentially. Exponential thinking is thinking so big that you know the vision cannot be accomplished by human effort alone. Unless God steps in, you will fail. It is the faith factor. It is what drives you to greater prayer effort and dependence on God. Here are some biblical examples of exponential thinking: 'Oh that you would burst from the heavens and come down! How the mountains would quake in your presence. As fire causes wood to burn and water to boil your coming would make the nations tremble' (Isaiah 64:1–2 NLT); 'Now to him who is able to do immeasurably more than all we ask or imagine, according to his power that is at work within us, to him be glory in the church and in Christ Jesus throughout all generations, for ever and ever!' (Ephesians 3:20–21); 'Finally, brothers and sisters, pray for us that the message of the Lord may spread rapidly and be honoured, just as it was with you' (2 Thessalonians 3:1 NIV Incl.).

Sometimes I think that modern-day Christians are just too easily satisfied. A few extra folk in our church and we (rightly) rejoice. But are we too quickly and easily satisfied? God wants so much more of his church. God is 'not wanting anyone to perish, but everyone to come to repentance' (2 Peter 3:9). There is a compelling sense of urgency in the New Testament that is not always present in the modern church.

In Western culture many churches are in decline, and 'business as usual' is not working. It is time to think differently. It is time to think exponentially.

Gerard Kelly, Pastor of Crossroads International Church in Amsterdam, and a well-known author and preacher, says, 'We should not be afraid to grow large, gathered churches, as islands of missional resource in a post-Christendom desert.' He continues, 'We will not mobilise millions of Europeans for the gospel without a number – a significant number – of large scale gathered communities.' Kelly reminds us that 'there is huge scope for partnership especially between the two groups characterised by Stuart Murray as, on the one hand "Emerging churches" and on the other hand "Inherited"'. He goes on:

> But it is only the larger churches that are able to amass the resources needed to feed missional initiatives. These churches are increasingly becoming the 'hubs' of missional networks – able to offer the training and leadership needed by fledging mission initiatives.[1]

What makes a church strategic?

1. A well-defined mission: a church that has a keen sense of mission and purpose that encompass both local and global mission.
2. Strong, competent leadership: leaders who have a commitment to long-term ministry.
3. A deep sense of community and fellowship: the belief in the value of one another's company and the significance of the family of faith.
4. A genuine resolve to make prayer a priority.
5. Increasing standards of commitment by church members involved in the ministries of the church.
6. A focus on celebration in worship.

---

[1] Gerard Kelly, *Christianity Magazine*, April 2006, p. 63.

7. Intentional evangelism.
8. The mobilising, equipping and training of volunteers through a systematic approach to gift discovery and involvement in ministry.
9. High visibility of the ministry in the local community.
10. Exponential thinking.

Exponential thinking is about participating in what God is doing. The disciples prayed exponentially after they had been forbidden to 'speak or teach at all in the name of Jesus' (Acts 4:18). Their bold prayer is recorded later in that same chapter of Acts:

> Now, Lord, consider their threats and enable your servants to speak your word with great boldness. Stretch out your hand to heal and perform miraculous signs and wonders through the name of your holy servant Jesus. After they prayed, the place where they were meeting was shaken. And they were all filled with the Holy Spirit and spoke the word of God boldly. (Acts 4:29–31)

God answered their courageous prayer. God honours this kind of thinking and faith. This participation with God can be described as living in the present in light of the future. This is exactly what Jesus did. His miracles were a demonstration of the presence of the kingdom of God, the kingdom that had come in Jesus but was yet to come fully. Jesus taught us to pray, 'your kingdom come, your will be done on earth as it is in heaven' (Matthew 6:10). The disciples had finally come to understand this, and after Pentecost, when they were all filled with the Holy Spirit, they began to live as Jesus lived, in the present in light of the future. This is what the church is called to do. Sadly, too many churches in the West now live in the present in light of past glories, instead of living in the present in light of future glories.

Jesus took the present seriously, and so must we, but he dealt with it in light of the future in terms of what God wanted done and would do. And so must we. Jesus did not passively accept the 'status quo', and neither must we. God is always ahead of us, beckoning us forward. To participate with what God is doing and wants done is to think exponentially. After all, as we have noted, he is able to do 'immeasurably more than all we ask or imagine'.

The question is, are we willing to participate with God? Are we really intentional about being the body of Christ in the time and place where God has placed us? Are you ready to participate with God in the coming of the kingdom in your community? Can we as churches in the present-day cultures of our cities handle the present in light of the future, or will we persist in trying to hold on to the past and allow events to pass us by? Those who try to do that find themselves frustrated and disappointed. Those who participate with the God of the future as well as the present will find themselves in challenging situations, but ones that lead to new opportunities of ministry and mission.

So what are some of the practical steps that can be taken?

Encourage exponential thinking

Encourage exponential thinking in your church. If you haven't got a dream team in your church, begin to think about who might be on such a team. In every church there are dreamers – people who dream the dream – and there are detailers – people who implement the dream. A strategic church needs both dreamers and detailers.

Choose people who find it easy to think exponentially. They are usually people who dream and then move on to the next dream. They are not naturally implementers. Often in a local church they are sidelined simply as dreamers.

It is not always the case that the senior leader – pastor, vicar, minister – is the person who thinks exponentially. If as a leader you are not that kind of person, you will be wise to gather round you people who do dream and can imagine and envision what the future could be like. Even if you are the one who can think exponentially, you will be wise to gather round you other dreamers so that there is a team of people thinking exponentially about the future of the church. So the first step is to establish a team of those who can think exponentially.

X and the Greek alphabet

X (or *chi*) is the twenty-second letter of the Greek alphabet. It is the first letter of the name of Christ in Greek. The vision for your church comes from God. Christ is the head of the church, and we dream not for our own self-aggrandisement but for the glory of Christ. As we are reminded in Ephesians 3, 'to him be glory in the church and in Christ Jesus' (Ephesians 3:21).

The vision for your church comes from God. Bring onto your team those who genuinely want God's vision and want to glorify Christ. Avoid having on your team those who dream simply to draw attention to themselves. Those who find God's vision are those who ask him for it. They depend on him. God gives vision to those who pray.

Persevere with seeking the dream

Some dream teams give up too soon. Trying to get God's vision for your church seems at first exciting, and even maybe relatively easy, but as time goes by it requires commitment, time and energy. 'Vision is usually birthed out of a serious search for God's direction.'[2] Nehemiah says, 'For some days I mourned and fasted and prayed before the God of heaven' (Nehemiah 1:4). Getting God's vision takes time. The reason for this, as Dan Southerland reminds us, is that 'Vision is not just a destination: it is a journey.

---

[2] Dan Southerland, *Transitioning*, Zondervan 2000, p. 25.

Vision is not just a product: it is a process. Vision is not just the finish line: it is the whole race!'[3] He reminds us that 'Any business guru can tell you that research and development is a major part of producing a winning product.'[4]

Organise the dream

Organise the vision into steps that people can understand. Sometimes the vision for the church is cast in too vague a manner, or it is too big for some people to take seriously, and they need help in understanding it. As the vision took time to be birthed, so it also takes time to be understood and accepted.

Don't rush the process of sharing the vision. The vision must be fully formed before sharing it with the whole church. You will need to show to your church that the vision has been thought through. Take them through it step by step.

Take time over the process. Don't rush people. Share the vision in as many different ways as possible. People learn in different ways – some by hearing, some by reading and some by watching.

Some key ways in which to communicate the vision are through preaching, through small groups where people have the opportunity to ask questions, through symbols and slogans that help people to remember the dream, through well-designed and well-made banners, and most of all through leaders modelling the vision. Visions are caught more than taught.

Nurture the dream

Allow God to continue to build it. Vision is an ongoing process. The dream will take into consideration: the New Testament principles and purposes of the church; the local community in which

---

[3] *Ibid.*, p. 20.
[4] *Ibid.*, p. 21.

your particular local church is placed (gain as much local information as possible – see Chapter 9); the make-up of your church;
and also its global perspective. Aim eventually for a document
describing the dream and containing information about the
church and the community.

Part of the process of establishing vision and direction for the
local church is an openness to learn from others. Other people
who are not necessarily part of the dream team may nevertheless
have a contribution to make. Spend time reflecting on what has
been developed. Commenting on the story of Nehemiah, Dan
Southerland reminds us that there was a four-month time lapse
between chapters 1 and 2 of the story. Southerland says, 'Vision
is usually given to those who wait patiently for it.'

Enlarge the vision

This is when we really begin to think exponentially. Rick Warren
puts this very simply when he says that the way to think exponentially is to add a nought. Rick tells the story of how he
believed that God wanted him to reach 3,000 people through
small groups. Then one day God told him that his dream was too
small and that he should add a nought. This meant that Rick was
now thinking about 30,000 people in small groups. How could
that possibly be accomplished? This brings you not only to the
point of faith but also to some hard thinking. A big vision forces
us to think creatively. Rick and his team faced the big question:
'How could they find enough leaders for so many people?' It was
at this moment that they came up with the idea of video-based
teaching. Rick would record the lesson for each house group on a
20-minute video, and as long as a person was willing to be a host,
then it was possible for a small group to gather and be taught and
have an opportunity for discussion. We now know that not only
did that method of teaching reach thousands of homes in the

community around the Saddleback Community Church, but it also enabled the book *The Purpose Driven Life* to be studied by small groups all over the world. All of this can be traced back to the moment when Rick heard God say, 'Add a nought.' You may limit the growth of your church if you do not enlarge the vision and set a goal so big that you are forced to think in new ways.

Notify key people

Notify other leaders and/or key people in the church of the way the thinking is developing. People like to be in on the early stages of a new journey. There comes a right time to share the vision with others. When Nehemiah went to Jerusalem to look at the ruined city, he said, 'I set out during the night with a few men. I had not told anyone what my God had put in my heart to do for Jerusalem' (Nehemiah 2:12).

Transfer the vision into a readable document

Transferring the vision into an easily readable document will help you to fine-tune it, to reflect on it and pray about it as you begin to share it with others. Keep the document as simple and brief as possible so that it doesn't get stuck in heavy theology and bureaucracy. Work together to sharpen the vision. Help those who are cautious about the vision to understand and own it. Know the difference between dreamers and detailers. Both kinds of people are important to the process.

Illustrate the vision

Help people to see the vision and not just read about it. Paint word-pictures of the needs of the local community and how the church could meet those needs. Paint word-pictures of what the church could be like in five or ten years' time. Encourage new Christians to tell their story so that people can see how the church is already working. Have someone make a video of the local community and its needs. If a new building is involved, then of course draw pictures of the proposed building.

Accommodate the doubters

Accommodate the doubters and the cautious. Such people are equally part of the church and are there by God's grace. We need them, and they are part of the team. God can speak through them to refine the vision. Give unenthusiastic people time to think through the vision and its implications for change. Do everything possible to help them understand the direction you believe the church should be going in, but at the same time you cannot allow them to set the agenda for the future of the church.

Limit the dreaming time

Limit the amount of time spent forming the dream. As much as it is important not to rush the process, at the same time constant procrastination breeds discouragement and frustration. Remember the example given earlier, when a leader said, 'Our existing vision has been in place for 10 years. It now seems dated. How can we build on it?' It's difficult to build on a vision that is ten years old. Procrastination can destroy the dream.

Talk up the vision

If the leaders are not excited and enthusiastic about it, then perhaps no one else will be. 'If the trumpet does not sound a clear call, who will get ready for battle?' (1 Corinthians 14:8). The pulpit is the most powerful tool for communicating the vision.

Humbly share the vision

Share the vision with humility and give God the credit. When you are excited and enthusiastic it is easy to be misunderstood. In some churches it is not easy for leaders to sound confident without being accused of being arrogant. 'Almost any pastor who tries to serve God in a biblical way is constantly faced with two classic dilemmas . . . being both humble and powerful and being both a servant and a leader.'[5] 'The apostle Paul on many occasions referred to himself as a servant. Yet his authority was awesome. He saw no contradiction in being simultaneously a servant of Jesus Christ and an apostle.'[6] In some European cultures it is particularly difficult to take the lead and share the vision, because that is immediately perceived as the leader drawing attention to him- or herself. Simply be sensitive to the way in which people may interpret the manner in which you present the vision. There is no need to dampen your enthusiasm or reduce the vision, but present it with genuine humility and modesty.

There are strategic churches where the leadership is strong and holds extraordinary authority, but the people never perceive their leaders as authoritarian. Instead the people enjoy the leadership. These leaders have learned how to combine humility with power and servant-heartedness with confidence. If the vision is of God, the devil will be quick to try to defeat it and will use every tactic there is, including causing people to misunderstand you.

Invoke God's blessing

Invoke God's blessing on the vision and everything about it. Ask God to bless his vision, not yours. His vision will prosper. He will

---

[5] C. Peter Wagner, *Leading Your Church to Growth*, MARC Europe, p. 80.

[6] *Ibid.*, p. 86.

provide you with the strength to complete it. He will send you the right people at the right time to support you. If it is God's vision and you are willing to implement it, it will not lack God's resources. As already stated, vision is birthed out of a serious search for God's direction. At every stage of exponential thinking, a key part of the strategy is to ask for the wisdom that God wants to give generously to those who ask him for it.

Name the dream

There comes a moment when the leader or leaders say, 'This is it. This is the dream. This is the vision we believe that God has given us.'

This vision may be so big that you know that unless God completes it, it will never be completed. I believe some leaders are gifted by God with enough faith to be incredibly confident that their vision has come from him. Such leadership is rare, but when it appears on the scene it captures attention and brings glory to God. In 1980 at the very first service of the Saddleback Community Church, in front of 60 people, Pastor Rick Warren stood and confidently shared this dream:

It is the dream of a place where the hurting, the depressed, the frustrated, and the confused can find love, acceptance, help, hope, forgiveness, guidance, and encouragement.

It is the dream of sharing the Good News of Jesus Christ with the hundreds of thousands of residents in south Orange County.

It is the dream of welcoming 20,000 members into the fellowship of our church family – loving, learning, laughing, and living in harmony together.

It is the dream of developing people to spiritual maturity through Bible studies, small groups, seminars, retreats, and a Bible school for our members.

It is the dream of equipping every believer for a significant ministry by helping them discover the gifts and talents God gave them.

It is the dream of sending out hundreds of career missionaries and church workers all around the world, and empowering every member for a personal life mission in the world. It is the dream of sending our members by the thousands on short-term mission projects to every continent. It is the dream of starting at least one new daughter church every year.

It is the dream of at least fifty acres of land, on which will be built a regional church for south Orange County – with beautiful, yet simple, facilities including a worship center seating thousands, a counseling and prayer center, classrooms for Bible studies and training lay ministers, and a recreation area. All of this will be designed to minister to the local person – spiritually, emotionally physically, and socially – and set in a peaceful, inspiring garden landscape.

I stand before you today and state in confident assurance that these dreams will become reality. Why? Because they are inspired by God.

Rick was confident that this vision would be fulfilled because he knew it was not his vision: it was God's.

At the 25th anniversary of the church, in 2005, before a packed Angel Stadium in California, Rick stood and said, 'That dream has been fulfilled.'

By anybody's judgement the story of the Saddleback Church is an incredible one that has changed the lives of thousands near it and influenced thousands more around the globe, bringing global glory to God.

Keep up the momentum

However long it may take to present the dream and for people to understand it and own it, a key part of the strategy is to keep up the momentum as the vision unfolds and is implemented. Not only is it true that if you take too long on the dream, enthusiasm diminishes, but also if the momentum is not sustained, then the dream is in danger of dying.

Keep up the momentum with reminders in bulletins and through testimonies, video clips, prayer times and small group discussion. Be careful not to tire people with the dream but be creative in using fresh ideas to present it. Keep the dream fresh and alive.

Involve and influence

Involve and influence key members of the church. These may or may not be appointed workers and leaders. They may be people whom others look to for guidance, people who are respected for their spiritual maturity. Such people are often unappointed leaders of others. They are supporters and encouragers of the leadership of the church. Because of their authenticity and maturity, they deserve your time and attention. This is not a political move, but a simple recognition that God has placed within your congregation people to help you get the job done, people who will support and encourage you. Not everybody in the church by any means is of sufficient spiritual character to have this influential role. It is perfectly correct that such people might influence others who find it hard to assimilate information and make decisions.

Narrow the gap between the future and the present

You may not know how God is going to complete this vision for your church. But you will know some things, and you will know some of the first steps in the process to making the dream a reality. Begin to demonstrate the possibilities now. Give small examples of what might be in the future. Learn to build on your existing strengths. There are some things that your church is already doing well. Imagine what might happen if they were being done better.

Glorify God

Exponential thinking is to bring honour to God. It is not about us. It is not even about our church. It is all about him and his church. Repeatedly express glory to God throughout the whole process, in celebrations of worship, in times of prayer, in letters and bulletins, in human stories. Wherever possible, intentionally give glory to God.

> Christ loved the church and gave himself up for her to make her holy, cleansing her by the washing with water through the word, and to present her to himself as a radiant church, without stain or wrinkle or any other blemish but holy and blameless. (Ephesians 5:25–27)

Whatever its shape or expression, a local church should be a Christian community where Christ is acknowledged as head and where God is glorified.

8

Generous Attitude

Many strategic churches are characterised by a very generous attitude. The model for this is the magnificently generous church in Jerusalem which began on the day of Pentecost: 'All the believers were together and had everything in common. Selling their possessions and goods, they gave to anyone who had need' (Acts 2:44–45 NIV Incl.). 'There were no needy persons among them. For from time to time those who owned lands or houses sold them, brought the money from the sales and put it at the apostles' feet, and it was distributed to anyone who had need' (Acts 4:34–35 NIV Incl.). There is no doubt that God expects his people to be generous. A healthy strategic church is a generous church. Therefore building an attitude of generosity should be part of the strategy. Here are some strategic steps towards becoming a generous church; and the first one is obvious!

Give outside the church

Endeavour to become known as a giving church. This is in direct contrast to, and the exact opposite of, what many non-churchgoers think today. Mention the church to some people, and visions of oversized thermometers outside ancient buildings appealing for money to repair the walls or the roof come to mind. Part of our strategy is to change the way people think about the church.

Giving reflects the character of God. 'For you know the grace of our Lord Jesus Christ, that though he was rich, yet for your sakes he became poor, so that you through his poverty might become rich' (2 Corinthians 8:9). The Bible tries to persuade us to be generous. 'But just as you excel in everything – in faith, in speech, in knowledge, in complete earnestness, and in your love for us – see that you also excel in this grace of giving' (2 Corinthians 8:7). Work towards becoming a generous church, not just for the sake of it but because this is who we should be.

Encourage rather than compel

Encourage your people to be generous. The Bible is full of helpful advice:

> Remember this: Whoever sows sparingly will also reap sparingly, and whoever sows generously will also reap generously. Each of you should give what you have decided in your heart to give, not reluctantly or under compulsion, for God loves a cheerful giver.' (2 Corinthians 9:6–7 NIV Incl.)

That passage does a number of things. First of all, it motivates us to be generous: 'whoever sows generously will also reap generously'. Then it says that we should not put people under pressure to give. People should not give 'reluctantly or under compulsion'. We should encourage people to give. Finally, it says we should show people the results of generosity: 'whoever sows generously will also reap generously'. The Bible is very clear that it is up to each person to decide how generous they are going to be. God wants people deliberately to choose to be generous. He loves cheerful givers.

Nominate projects for support

Nominate certain projects each year that the church can support. A church anniversary is a good occasion to invite people to contribute to a thanksgiving offering so that that money can be given away to help others.

Some churches become well known for their generosity. Here are two completely different examples. First, the Willow Creek Community Church in South Chicago has a car ministry, supplying renovated cars to people who need them but can't afford them.

> There's a ministry of auto mechanics who decided on their own to get together twice a week and repair the cars of single moms for free. In fact, many people at Willow Creek don't trade in their old car when they buy a new one. Instead they donate it to the church, and the mechanics fix it up and give it to a family that's desperate for transportation. In a recent two-year period, the church distributed nearly seventy cars.[1]

Secondly, in the UK a Baptist church in Grays, Essex, started serving those outside the church by providing clothing for families in need. This became such a strong feature that the church became known as 'the church with the black-sack ministry'. They also provided holidays for single-parent families, many of whom were referred to the church by Social Services and other agencies.

Projects can be community based or thousands of miles away in other countries. In 2004, Frinton Free Church raised enough finance to construct four church buildings in India where people would never have been able to afford to build their own. But it's not just in these kinds of project that the church can demonstrate a generous attitude. There are other ways, too, as we shall now see.

---

[1] Lynne and Bill Hybels, *Rediscovering Church*, Zondervan 1995, p. 162.

Entertain the local community

Entertain guests. The Bible says, 'Practise hospitality' (Romans 12:13). For example, why not hold a dinner for people who serve the community, such as the local police, fire-fighters, ambulance personnel, health visitors, refuse collectors, etc.? Invite them to a meal and say, 'This is just to say thank you for the way in which you serve our community.' This is a way of showing love and care for the community, and for people whose jobs are often taken for granted.

A strategic church is a hospitable church.

Research new ways to be generous

Generosity is not just about money. We can also be generous with time, energy and skills. 'The generous prosper and are satisfied: those who refresh others will themselves be refreshed' (Proverbs 11:25 NLT). The Christian church is the largest volunteer force in the country. It is a massive resource of information, skill and friendship. Sometimes all people want is time:

> You are generous because of your faith. And I am praying that you will really put your generosity to work, for in so doing you will come to an understanding of all the good things we can do for Christ. (Philemon 1:6 NLT)

Offer help to those in need

Take the initiative to be generous. Don't wait to be asked. But don't be taken by surprise if sometimes generosity is not accepted. Some people find it more difficult to receive than to give. And as mentioned in Chapter 1, although the church is a sign of hope to the world, through its example and service to others, it is also, for some, the world's enemy, often persecuted and despised. Nevertheless, the church should always be first on the scene when there is a human need. We should be the Good Samaritan rather than the priest and Levite who passed by on the other side, with seemingly more important duties to attend to.

Unleash the joy of giving

When the apostle Paul is writing to the church in Corinth about their gift for needy Christians in Jerusalem, he says this:

> (God) will give you many opportunities to do good, and he will produce a great harvest of generosity in you. Yes, you will be enriched so that you can give even more generously, and when we take your gifts to those who need them, they will break out in thanksgiving to God. So two things will happen – the needs of the Christians in Jerusalem will be met, and they will joyfully express their thanksgiving to God. You will be glorifying God through your generous gifts. For your generosity to them will prove that you are obedient to the good news of Christ. (2 Corinthians 9:10–14 NLT)

Once again we see that generosity is a choice. It is not something that happens automatically necessarily. Those Christians in Corinth chose to be generous. If you are a leader, why not find ways to unleash the joy of generosity and encourage people to make this choice?

Seize new opportunities

Seize opportunities to be generous. Sometimes opportunities to be generous present themselves at very short notice. The obvious example is when there is a sudden crisis of need somewhere in the world as a result of an earthquake, drought, conflict or other cause. The church therefore needs to be ready at any time, which means it continually lives in a state of generosity.

Ask individuals to be generous

Leaders have a responsibility under God to ask people to be generous. This means not only appealing to a congregation but also to certain individuals who have been entrusted with the responsibility of wealth. God has strong words to say to those who hoard wealth for themselves: 'Your wealth has rotted . . . Your gold and silver are corroded . . . You have hoarded wealth' (James 5:2–3).

> Command those who are rich in this present world not to be arrogant nor to put their hope in wealth, which is so uncertain, but to put their hope in God, who richly provides us with everything for our enjoyment. Command them to do good, to be rich in good deeds, and to be generous and willing to share. (1 Timothy 6:17–18)

Help people to understand that they have been blessed in order to be a blessing. Why not challenge them to give away something valuable to someone they would like to bless? Make sure it isn't something collecting dust in an attic or garage. Give away your best. People will be blown away by your gracious generosity.

Thank people for their generosity

Do not take generosity for granted. Receiving thanks should not be the motive for giving, but it is right that gratitude towards those who give should be expressed. Be generous with gratitude.

Testify to God's goodness

Affirm God's goodness and faithfulness. 'God loves a cheerful giver. And God is able to make all grace abound to you, so that in all things at all times, having all that you need, you will abound in every good work' (2 Corinthians 9:7–8).

There will be those in the church who have given in faith and have discovered that they are not able to out-give God. Encourage people to tell their stories of God's faithfulness. This strengthens the faith of others and brings honour to God.

Illustrate generosity by sharing stories

Give examples to the congregation of what happens when people are generous. Share the stories. Let's look at two examples.

When Frinton Free Church provided buildings for churches in India, the following story appeared in *Decision* magazine:

> In 2004 when Frinton Free Church decided to do something for those in the developing world, the congregation decided to think big and said, 'Let's build a church for a congregation in India'. (In India a church building to house a small congregation can be built for just a few thousand pounds.) And so for their church's anniversary gift-day they decided to put the money raised towards this project. Their minister, the Rev David Beer, even dared to dream 'wouldn't it be wonderful if we could build two church buildings, at £6,250 each. . .'. Incredibly, a staggering £25,000 was raised! This was enough to buy not just one church building – it was enough to buy FOUR.[2]

From Willow Creek's car ministry comes the following story:

> When I became my son's sole supporter, we had nothing – only our clothes, no car, no house, no child support. I was fortunate to find a job a mile and a half away from the apartment so I could walk to work. People seemed to rally around and help me from time to time by lending me their cars so I could hold down a second part-time job that paid the bills the primary job couldn't.
>
> I learned to live day by day, grateful for each car I drove, grateful to Willow Creek for introducing me to Christ, grateful to the youth ministries for being a 'father' to my son, grateful for the church's Rebuilders Ministry, which taught me that God would be my husband and so much more.

---

[2] *Decision: Samaritan's Purse*, November/December 2004, BGEA, p. 25.

Our lives have changed in miraculous ways because of this church – because people reach out and touch others in ways that feel to us like being touched by God.

I wanted you to know how hard it is to be a single mom. We don't know how to fix things when they break, and often there is no money to have them fixed by someone, so we limp along, praying for the car we're driving to get us safely where we need to go 'just one more time'. I've lived with the 'just one more time' prayer longer than I can remember and am amazed that God honoured that prayer for so long.

I can hardly take it all in that I should be the recipient of this car you have provided. I want to cry every time I get in it. It feels to me like another 'loaner' car – but this time it's a loaner from Jesus. I'm driving His car. I feel blessed again and am a witness of how He gives 'good things' to His children.[3]

Trust God with money

Generosity and faith are partners. Although generosity includes more than finance, nevertheless God chooses money as a means of enabling us to show our commitment to him. For example, in the Old Testament the people of Israel were told to bring a tenth of their produce before God as a way of honouring him:

Bring this tithe to eat before the Lord your God at the place he shall choose as his sanctuary: this applies to your tithes of grain, new wine, olive oil, and the first-born of your flocks and herds. The purpose of tithing is to teach you always to put God first in your lives. (Deuteronomy 14:23 Living Bible Paraphrase)

Both at an individual and at a church level we are called to trust God with our finances.

Understand ungenerous people

Understand those who find generosity or giving difficult. There is nothing worse than someone feeling constantly pressured to give.

[3] Lynne and Bill Hybels, *Rediscovering Church*, Zondervan 1995, pp. 162–63.

They may not have grown up in a tradition of generosity. In every church there are pensioners, people who are on a fixed income, people who are unemployed and people who are facing financial difficulties. Some will argue that tithing is the great leveller. Whether you have a hundred pounds or ten pounds, the proportion that you give is the same. However, the Bible makes it very clear that each person should give what they have decided in their heart to give, not under outside pressure, for God loves a willing and cheerful giver.

Devote time to this subject

Give time to study the subject of giving and to developing a generous Christian community. This will involve prayer, Bible study and the working-out of an intentional strategy that will include many of the principles outlined above and encourage people to give.

Embrace a generous spirit

Let your church be known for its generosity. Paul's letter to the Romans talks about the various gifts that people have within the Christian community. At one point he talks about the gift of giving. He says if someone's gift 'is contributing to the needs of others, then give generously' (Romans 12:8 NIV Incl.).

Don't suppress those who want to be generous and who have a particular gift of contributing to the needs of others. As we said at the beginning of this chapter, generosity doesn't come automatically to every person. Perhaps it should to Christians, but the reality is that, for many of us, this is an area of our Christian living that needs to be worked on and developed.

A generous church full of generous people is well on the way to becoming a strategic church.

9

Involvement with the Local Community

The previous chapters have defined the church as a Christian community where Christ is acknowledged as head and where God is glorified. But it is more than that. Some years ago, J. H. Oldham, then a well-known Anglican theologian, gave this vivid definition of the church: 'Jesus Christ at work in the world through the fellowship of redeemed sinners.' It is an astonishing thought that Jesus Christ chooses ordinary people who have become his followers to make his presence known in the community and world.

One of the most visible and significant features of a strategic church is its involvement in the community. This can range from identifying and supporting local initiatives designed to build a healthy community environment, to partnering other agencies as well as other churches for the total well-being of the community. It can also mean getting down into some of the pain and hurt of people in need. A strategic church will witness to a holistic gospel. The love of Christ demands this.

Involvement in the local community is not optional for churches. Until relatively recently, much of the written material about the social involvement of the local church had a global emphasis through mission and aid agencies – caring for the poor, feeding the hungry, standing alongside the disenfranchised, directing energy and finance overseas. This is an essential emphasis, but it starts at the level of the local community. There are churches that have become well known for their support of overseas mission, but some of them have been almost completely uninvolved locally. In fact, for some Christians mission has been simply equated with overseas support. In more recent years the balance has started to be redressed. In some churches the pendulum may have swung too far!

'Making disciples' takes into account the social dimensions of the gospel. It is a tragedy to sever evangelism from social concern and action. Such division has been described as a twentieth-century aberration. One of the tragedies of the last century, especially in America, was the so-called 'modernist versus fundamentalist' controversy.

The 'modernists' were concerned about meeting the social needs of people, but this was often at the expense of evangelism.

> In reaction to these views, the fundamentalists, or conservative evangelicals, who understood the centrality and the priority of evangelisation, equated a diminution of evangelistic commitment and evangelical theology with social action. Thus, they (the fundamentalists) gave themselves almost exclusively to seeing people brought to faith in Christ as they reacted to the modernist's motif of the faith.[1]

The same problem existed to a lesser extent in the UK and Europe. Many Christians became disenchanted with the emphasis on just the verbal communication of the gospel. It seemed as though the church talked so much about the 'message' of reconciliation that it neglected the 'ministry' of reconciliation. Both in America and Europe the imbalance seems now to be less.

Earlier evangelicals knew no such division. History is full of examples of evangelical involvement in the wider needs of men and women. C. H. Spurgeon is remembered not only as a great

---

[1] Lewis A. Drummond, *Ripe for Harvest*, Broadman Press 2001, pp. 129–30.

gospel preacher, but also as someone who had a passionate concern for social welfare. He built orphanages and almshouses, pioneered evening classes and founded a college. Charles Finney, the great American evangelist, was also a fervent abolitionist and social activist. William Wilberforce is credited with ending Britain's role in the slave trade. John Wesley, strong for abolition, also started medical clinics and financial credit unions for the poor. We can recall the social work of men like William Booth, Robert Raikes, Lord Shaftesbury and many others. Even the modern Labour Party in Britain grew out of evangelical concern. As someone has said, 'May God revive his churches and put them on the trail of needy people. May the Holy Spirit lay a true burden for a lost and broken world on all hearts.'[2]

Many churches still need a powerful move of the Holy Spirit before the membership will get involved in meeting the needs of the community in a holistic fashion. This is not because of theology, but through either not knowing how to be involved or apparently lacking time. Many Christians know that the church should connect pragmatically with the community but believe they are too busy to do so. It is truly amazing how unhurried and half-hearted some Christians can be about problems that do not immediately affect their own well-being. Some Christians do live very busy lives. This is a leader's typical dilemma. There is no easy answer to this, which is why larger churches tend to be staff-led. But to inspire and motivate is a leadership role.

Here are some steps that may help your church to get involved in the community.

Champion the community

Of all the groups that should champion the good of the community, the church should be taking a leading role. Be prepared to

---

[2] Lewis A. Drummond, *The Word of the Cross*, Broadman 1992, p. 295.

stand up for the local community, to give a supporting voice to all that is good and wholesome. Work hard at enabling the community to have confidence in the church. A strategic church is one where the community knows that the church will always champion the cause of the community. It is a safe place that people can turn to for support. This calls for a relational strategy, where the church builds relationships with individuals as well as with groups. This, of course, is a gradual process over a period of many months or even years. Building up the confidence of the community in the church takes time.

There was a time when more than a few churches would not entertain taking either the wedding or the funeral service of a non-churchgoer. Some still do not. I remember a young couple coming to my door having visited three previous churches in the hope of getting married in church. They were not churchgoers. I invited them in for a conversation. They then told me that I was the first minister actually to invite them in – they never got beyond the threshold of the three previous churches (of varying denominations)! After several conversations, and many months later, the couple were married in our church. They later came to faith, were baptised and became enthusiastic workers in the church. Their story became known to others in the community and resulted in unchurched people understanding our church in a much more positive light.

On another occasion we were asked to visit an unchurched family where a teenage boy had suddenly died, and the family wanted a funeral in our church. On the day of the funeral the church was packed with hundreds of local unchurched people, including many teenagers who had no church connection. These situations are not to be abused. They are opportunities to show care and support. The parents of the young man concerned eventually became Christians and church members and were influential among many of their unchurched friends.

These are just two simple examples of ways in which to connect with the local community and begin to build confidence in the church. Many leaders reading this will identify with these examples. The situations I have described are just two steps in the long process of winning the community, but two very important steps. There are many other similar opportunities to make contact with the community which will come to you over a period of time.

There are always opportunities to build relationships and show love and care with no strings attached. One of the things that excited people so much in Jesus' day was that he seemed to care for people and was interested in them in precisely that manner. He had no angle, unlike so many of the religious people of his day. In the same way we should have no angle when we help people.

Earlier in this book we mentioned that Jesus told his disciples to be 'as shrewd as snakes and innocent as doves' (Matthew 10:16). Don't manipulate people to your own ends, and don't abuse the God-given opportunities. Our attitude should be like that of the Good Samaritan who helped simply because someone was in need. That should always be our motive. People quickly discover if our motive is self-centred. We need to build healthy relationships in the community to enable their confidence in the local church to grow. Jesus did this all the time. Like him, we do not condone every behaviour, and we do not compromise our message, but neither do we reject people or turn them away. While preaching on that well-known parable of the Good Samaritan, the great civil rights leader Dr Martin Luther King Jr said, 'I should like to talk with you about a good man, whose exemplary life will always be a flashing light to plague the dozing conscience of mankind.'[3]

---

[3] Martin Luther King Jr, *Strength to Love*, Fontana 1970, p. 26.

Champion the cause of the community. Champion the cause of the disadvantaged and the marginalised.

There are Christian organisations that can help the church connect with the local community. In the UK one of these is Faithworks: 'Faithworks is a movement of thousands of individuals, churches and organisations motivated by their Christian faith to serve the needs of their local communities and positively influence society as a whole.' (Contact details can be found under the Resources section at the end of this book.)

Observe the culture

Observe the life and culture of the local community. As the Holy Spirit begins to motivate church members to get involved in their local community, the first step is to begin to discover and understand community needs. This cannot be done in a hurry. Building a strategy for getting involved in the local community must begin with gathering information. Much of this will come through simple observation. Actions such as walking the streets of the neighbourhood, taking time to talk to people, talking to local businesses and regularly reading the local newspaper are obvious ways in which to gather information.

A local council Internet site can provide information, such as the average age of the community, the number of people employed in it, the number unemployed, and what the latest community trends are. The same or similar information would no doubt be available at a local library. The church should be an expert on the community and should know and understand the community as much as, or even better than, any other group.

The local council Internet site will include the Community Strategy for your area. This is prepared by the Local Strategic Partnership, consisting of various organisations in the community. The following is an example:

'Working in partnership to enhance the quality of life for residents of the Tendring District'.

In 2000 all councils were given statutory responsibility to prepare a Community Strategy setting out how the social, economic and environmental well-being of the residents of their area could be improved. In Tendring the statutory, business and community agencies came together to tackle issues such as regeneration, crime and disorder, health and the environment.

The Community Strategy is produced by the Local Strategic Partnership (LSP) and provides a framework for regeneration and service improvement by setting out their priorities over the next six years.[4]

Your church, or your local network of churches, is able to have representation on this partnership. In many parts of the UK local churches enjoy an active and effective role in the shaping of their community.

For example, Faithworks Poole . . . embarked upon a programme of care for vulnerable elderly people in the town. Their involvement with the Poole Partnership has meant that the project's volunteers have been able to be trained by the Pensions Agency, giving them a much deeper understanding of the statutory help available to their clients. Without the partnership, this link, and the resulting breadth of service, would probably never have been possible.

(For more on Faithworks, see Appendix 5.)

If you haven't already done so, it may be helpful to make a survey of your community. There are four steps that you could take:

1. Prepare a map of the community showing the area considered to be the church's responsibility.
2. Describe the area – type of housing, age of population, racial patterns, general culture, sub-cultural groups, income level, educational level, problems related to the environment. The

---

[4] Tendring District Council website.

demographics of the area are vital to have. Discover the future of the community as well as the present.

3. Describe those community needs that could be met by the church.

4. Evaluate the effectiveness of the church in meeting the needs of the community. What can and should be done to meet those needs? What future needs can be anticipated and prepared for?[5]

Collect and study information about your church as well as the surrounding community. How long has your church been in existence? Why was it started? Who started it? Why is it located where it is? What has been its journey so far – its history? What has been its previous philosophy of church and understanding of mission? Chart its progress through the years in terms of growth and decline. Answers to these questions will give clues to the congregation's expectations of the future. Are those expectations correct? Can they be changed? Should they be changed?

Map your community

Draw a map of your community. Decide what area is your responsibility. It may be your parish, in which case the boundaries of your community are easily defined. If you are not a parish church, you may have to define your community by natural boundaries such as railways, rivers or main roads. You may decide that 'everyone within 15 or 20 minutes' walking distance of your church' defines your community. Mark on the map where members of your congregation are living.

Divide the community up into areas that can be prayed for by prayer teams, by people living in the area or by individual prayer

---

[5] David Beer, *50 Ways to Help Your Church Grow*, Kingsway Publications 2000, pp. 147–48.

champions. The important thing is to know your community, to pray for your community and to have a strategy to connect with the people in your community.

Multiply the good things

Multiply the good things that are happening in your community. Work with other churches and other agencies to multiply the effectiveness of the good things that are already happening.

The Faithworks movement is an excellent resource for helping churches work together with other agencies in the community. Malcolm Duncan, leader of Faithworks, has given permission for one of his articles to be reproduced in this book (see Appendix 5).

Uncover needs

Who are the poor and disadvantaged in your community? Who are the people who have recently moved into the area? Who are the people going through changes? Why not put together a new-home kit for those who have just moved into the area, a new baby kit for those who have just had a baby or a comfort kit for those who have lost a loved one? Think of things you can do for those who are grieving, for those who are depressed, for those who have lost their job. People are more open to the gospel when they are in a period of transition. One church developed transition kits to help their small groups reach out to their community where people are going through changes. There may be families who need work doing in their homes but can't afford it: they need help with cleaning, painting or repairs.

C. Peter Wagner makes a helpful distinction between 'social service' and 'social action'.[6] Although Wagner applies the distinction

---

[6] C. Peter Wagner, *Church Growth and the Whole Gospel*, MARC Europe 1981, p. 36.

to global ministry, it also applies to local ministry. 'Social service is the kind of social ministry geared to meet the needs of individuals and groups of persons in a direct and immediate way.' By this Wagner means that, if a house is burned down, social service will provide food for the family, temporary accommodation, help with refurnishing a new home, etc. This kind of ministry involvement provides food for the hungry in your community and lodging for the homeless. 'Social action is the kind of social ministry geared towards social structures.' The scope is broader and the effects more far-reaching. If a local council is ignoring the needs of a minority group in the community, social action tries to correct the injustice. It may mean lobbying the council or bringing the injustice to the attention of the rest of the community by using the local media. Wagner continues:

> The church does not have an option as to whether or not it will be involved in social ministry. The kingdom lifestyle demands it. But just how Christians individually and collectively become involved in social ministries is not set forth in the Bible, and therefore choices have to be made. One of these choices concerns the degree of involvement in social service and social action. While both are important, it should be recognised that a choice at this point will often affect the growth of the church or churches involved . . . Here is a church growth principle: *when churches are involved in social ministries, the churches which specialise in social service tend to attract more new members than the ones specialising in social action.*[7]

Negotiate with local leaders

In 'social service' and 'social action', if there are things requiring attention to meet needs or improve the local environment, and nobody seems to be doing anything about it, why not negotiate

---

[7] *Ibid.*, p. 37.

with local councillors or leaders of other organisations to mobilise teams? For example, you may need to help people become more environmentally aware. That may mean organising groups to discuss how the environment can be improved. An obvious need in many communities is simply to pick up litter, begin a recycling project or start a community garden.

One of the biggest needs in UK local communities that has recently been highlighted by the government is for a far greater understanding between the many different cultural groupings in UK cities and towns, particularly among those groups that could be described as having 'extreme' viewpoints. The church could have a vital role to play in bringing people together, helping them to understand each other and work together. Not every church could cope with this, but many do have the human resources and could provide community workers with this mandate.

Initiate new projects

If the church can pick up needs before anyone else, it means that whenever other agencies identify those needs, they find the Christian community is already there. That's where God would have us be – ahead of the crowd, pioneering the way, demonstrating kingdom values.

If there is no Internet café in the town, why not set one up? If one is not already in existence, start a 'feed the homeless' project. There are a number of examples where local churches have taken the initiative. For example, a Baptist church in Cambridge initiated a homeless project by turning its basement into accommodation for the homeless. They worked with local traders who helped provide food and general resources. They worked closely with local agencies and the council, and helped many hundreds of homeless men and women. The church won the confidence of many in the local community.

Trail some new ideas

Let the church become an ideas factory for ways in which the local community can be improved. In many areas the churches together form a significant group of volunteers. This group may well outnumber any other individual organisation and possess a rich wealth of creativity. Strategic churches are churches that take the lead and set the pace for the remainder of the community.

Working together as churches, together forming a Christian community for the town or village, accomplishes far more in creative thinking than working alone.

Yield to good things

Co-operate in good things that may already be happening in the community. For example, don't repeat what others are already doing. There is little need to do what the local council, another church or the Social Services are already doing, or some other charity within the community. It is better to join them and partner with them. No doubt they could use more support emotionally, more volunteers or more finance. This may be a way of seeing what God is already doing outside the church in the community and joining him in the work that is already going on.

Identify key people

Identify key people within the local community. They may include key business people, local councillors and leaders of residents' associations, as well as doctors, solicitors and leaders of other organisations. The message is, don't go it alone when there are other people in the community with whom you may be able to partner and whose skills and expertise you need.

Neutralise opposing views

Conflicts can arise within a community that may be sparked off by different political viewpoints. There are sometimes opposing points of view over planning applications, what to provide for young people, and, sadly, sometimes conflicts brought about by ethnic and racial differences. In some communities the church has a big part to play in bringing people together, helping people to understand each other and being what the Bible calls us to be – ministers of reconciliation.

Volunteer to be helpers

Volunteer to be helpers and workers for other agencies and projects. Outside agencies are often surprised when offers of further volunteer help come from the Christian churches. Again, this is a case of looking at the community, seeing what is being done and looking to see where the church can help further.

Organise inter-church teams

More is accomplished when people work together in teams than when they try to go it alone. Resist the temptation to work alone as one church in order to gain your church the credit. Strategic churches get involved in the community not to develop their own profile, as tempting as that is, but because there is work to be done. The church that doesn't care who gets the credit, as long as people are ministered to in the name of Christ, is the strategic church and the church that God uses.

In some towns in the UK, churches are working together to provide 'town' or 'street pastors'. These pastors receive training before they begin their ministry.

Loan resources to community projects

Loan people, equipment and buildings to local community projects. Normally churches are very good at allowing their buildings to be used by outside organisations. Inevitably there is always a risk involved, particularly where equipment is loaned. There are occasions when the church can lend volunteers for short-term projects, and also lend equipment or buildings on a short-term basis.

Vocalise community needs

If there are needs in the community that it generally hasn't recognised, it may be a ministry of the church to bring those needs to the attention of either the community as a whole or the local council. One of the ways to do this, of course, is through the local newspaper or, if it's a larger community, through local radio. Leaders from a local church can bring needs to the attention of their congregation even through preaching, but also through weekly notices and bulletins. Part of the responsibility of a local church is to identify needs within a community, and then to vocalise and draw people's attention to them.

Evaluate what has been done

Some churches are very good at identifying what needs to be done but slow to look back at what has been accomplished. Looking at what has been accomplished is often a way to motivate people to work in the present and to think about what more can be done. What has our church achieved in the community in the past ten years? What difference has our church made to the community over the past five years? Answers to these questions can sometimes be encouraging, and it is right to say thank you to people and give praise to God for what has been accomplished. Evaluation is always valuable and points to what can be learned from past experience.

Motivate volunteers

Motivation for Christians ultimately comes from Scripture. Encouragement and many of the processes and principles already mentioned in this book support that truth. Ultimately, 'You will be amazed what people do for Jesus that they will not do for your vision statement.'[8]

The parable of the Good Samaritan, mentioned earlier in this chapter, contains many profound principles. In answer to the question 'And who is my neighbour?' (Luke 10:29) Jesus told us to go and *be* a neighbour to others. At the end of the parable Jesus asks the question, 'Which of these three [the priest, the Levite or the Samaritan] do you think was a neighbour to the man who fell into the hands of robbers?' (Luke 10:36). The man who asked the original question answered, 'The one who had mercy on him' (Luke 10:37). 'Jesus told him, "Go and do likewise".' In other words, 'Go and do the same. Be a neighbour to those in need.'

Notice the quality at the heart of the story: mercy. We are to show mercy. That takes time. People today say they are short of time. We need to challenge them. We all have the same amount of time. It is how we use it that is the issue. The Samaritan was a busy person. He was on a journey. He had things to do. We know that because he gave the man who had been hurt to an innkeeper and said, 'Look after him . . . and when I return, I will reimburse you for any extra expense you may have' (Luke 10:35). The Samaritan had to move on. But in spite of whatever commitment he had, here was a man who noticed someone else in need.

---

[8] Neil Cole, *Organic Church*, Jossey-Bass/Wiley 2005.

Sometimes we don't notice others in need because we are living life at too fast a pace. To notice someone hurting, you have to slow down. The Samaritan stopped to help, even though he was on a journey that no doubt was important to him. We too need to be prepared to set aside our own agendas in order to help someone in need.

> In showing our love, no task should be too menial. Jesus specialised in acts of service most people try to avoid: washing feet, helping children, fixing [preparing] breakfast, and serving lepers. Nothing was beneath him, because his service flowed from his love.
>
> Jesus indicated our acts of love should be very practical; even giving a cup of cold water in his name is an act of love (Matthew 10:42). There are so many needs in the world; simply look around and begin to address what you see.[9]

Sometimes innovative ideas will motivate people. For example, you may not be able to have the kind of car ministry described above, but you could help a single parent or an elderly person by helping to look after their car, checking the air in the tyres, and checking the oil level and other fluids. The car could be washed and vacuumed, and if you really want to bless that person, you could fill up the car with petrol!

Empower with training

Empower volunteers. As already stated, people are more willing to volunteer if they feel equipped and resourced. More volunteers will be forthcoming if there is the offer of some relevant training and equipping. Further empower them by delegating responsibilities to them; authorise them to do the work that they have volunteered to do. Some people do not like responsibility, but others thrive on it.

---

[9] Rick Warren (ed.), *Better Together*, Purpose Driven Publishing 2004, pp. 61–62.

By now you may be thinking, 'How do we get all this started?' Answer: one step at a time. One of those steps could be to jump-start the church with a strategy such as 40 Days of Purpose or 40 Days of Community. During a period of 40 days a church can be significantly changed. Both these strategies are offered by the Purpose Driven movement. Thousands of churches all over the world have used them: 40 Days of Purpose is about renewal in the church; 40 Days of Community is about building a sense of community in the church, and then connecting with and getting involved in the community beyond the church. There may be similar projects that a church can use to enlist, motivate, mobilise and empower volunteers, but, having gained personal experience of these two 40-day journeys, I would join with many other churches in suggesting that these two strategies are among the most effective. In the context of this chapter I would urge you to look at 40 Days of Community.

This strategy consists of six Sunday messages that align with small group study and daily devotional reading. This power of alignment unifies the church. The heart of the small group work is for each small group to reach out to the community. The strategy calls for a 40-day commitment on the part of church members; people respond to a short-term commitment more readily than to a long-term one. Evidence, however, shows that having experienced a taste of this level of involvement in the church and the community, a significant number of people want to continue their commitment beyond the 40 days. This can lead to implementing material and resources from other organisations such as Faithworks.

Hopefully, it is the long term that leaders have in view for their churches, but people are helped by first experiencing a deeper level of commitment and involvement in the short term. Many churches who have experienced 40 Days of Community have said that their members want to continue.

Here are some church stories:

During 40 Days of Community over 90 per cent of the congregation of Jesmond Parish Church in Newcastle-upon-Tyne were involved in small groups which ran various mission projects, such as working with asylum seekers, homeless young mothers, student groups, and various evangelistic projects. The Senior Assistant Minister, the Revd Jonathan Redfearn, reported that 40 Days of Community also influenced the church's giving: 'the church is involved in a £1.6 million church plant project in Gateshead and by the end of 40 Days of Community [we] had £1.2 million.'

The Revd Carl Stokes, Minister of Hawkwell Baptist Church, and who also ran the campaign, reported that with each small group taking on both a ministry and mission project:

> we learned what it is to really love and care for each other in community and reach out to the wider community. It was fantastic to see many in the fellowship being empowered to show God's love to the local community in so many different and exciting ways, from gardening for the elderly to dog walking, to putting on a BBQ for the community, to decorating people's houses and to litter picking and so many other activities to declare that we love the people of Rochford.

He also reported that 18 of the 21 small groups continued beyond the campaign, a number of non-Christians and people who don't even attend the church being members of those groups. As a result of doing both 40 Days of Purpose and 40 Days of Community the church has grown from 62 members to 119 in the last 3 years.

Pastor Shaun Lambert of Stanmore Baptist Church reported that 'there wasn't huge numerical growth but there was growth in health. There was a lot more prayer going on, but the biggest impact seemed to be the small groups'. Shaun went on to say that 'most of the small groups took on projects both to bless the church and the neighbours – and they have become much more part of the mainstream of the church rather than little satellites'.

One church even said, before beginning 40 Days of Community, 'as far as our Church is concerned, this campaign has already been worthwhile, and we haven't publicly kicked off yet!'

Notify local authorities

It is always good to work in partnership with the local authorities. Let them see that the church is willing to be accountable. Make it part of your strategy to win the confidence of local authorities. In my experience I have worked with the police, the Social Services, the Fire Department, doctors and ambulance personnel, for the benefit of those we were trying to help. In some situations it is important that authorities such as the local police know what you are doing. For example, when a church I served as senior pastor was involved in helping young people break free from drug dependence, it often involved actually receiving the substances handed over by youth who wanted to break their drug dependence. The substances then had to be handed over to the police. This ministry became so extensive that a senior police officer commented, 'You are doing a better job of cleaning up this town than we are.' We had to keep them informed and in turn ask them to trust us, for we would not betray the confidence of the individuals we were helping.

Thank volunteers and give God the glory

Once again, as in other strategies, don't take people for granted. Thanking volunteers, the authorities and other organisations whom you have partnered helps to build healthy relationships within the community. However God may use you as 'ministers' and 'messengers' of reconciliation, thank other people and give him all the glory and the praise.

10

A Caring Heart

A caring heart is undoubtedly at the centre of a strategic church. No matter how strategic a church may be in other areas of its life, if it does not have a caring heart, then it will be ineffective as a fully functioning, strategic, biblical community. Fellowship and caring relationships are the heartbeat of a truly strategic church. According to the New Testament, the church is not just another organisation; it is not a club; and it is more than an institution. It is described in the New Testament as a fellowship, a family and a body – the body of Christ.

'Now you are no longer strangers to God and foreigners to heaven, but you are members of God's very own family, citizens of God's country, and you belong in God's household with every other Christian' (Ephesians 2:19, Living Bible paraphrase). The church is a family. Notice that it doesn't say that the church is *like* a family. It says the church *is* a family. It is a spiritual family in which God lives. The church is possessed of a divine energy: 'And in him you too are being built together to become a dwelling in which God lives by his Spirit' (Ephesians 2:22).

If the church is a family, then like any family there needs to be a sense of belonging: 'You belong in God's household with every other Christian.' Every church needs to develop this sense of belonging. That is why it is important to track the new arrivals, as mentioned in Chapter 6. The caring heart of the church needs to be discovered by newcomers at an early stage, particularly in the larger churches. Can a larger church have a sense of belonging? It most certainly can. A large church can have a caring heart and a sense of belonging without everybody necessarily knowing each other. It is not true that larger churches cannot have a sense of belonging and experience fellowship. Some larger churches of many thousands of members still manage to convey a strong sense of belonging. In contrast, some small churches can be so introverted that a sense of belonging only occurs after someone has been in the church for a prolonged period of time.

There is a difference between belonging and fellowship. Fellowship happens at a deeper level and therefore in a smaller group, which is why small groups are important in any church.

So a sense of belonging has nothing to do with the size of the church. It has everything to do with attitude, and especially the attitude of care. This is clearly spelt out in Philippians 2:1–5. Verse 5 says, 'Your attitude should be the same as that of Christ Jesus.'

Local churches need to emphasise strongly the importance of belonging to a local church family, because too many Christians today float from one church to another. As such they cannot be a vibrant part of the body of Christ which finds its expression in a commitment to a local fellowship. The difference between being a Christian and being a member of the church family is commitment.

The basis of the church family is relationships. The Bible says we are to treat each other like members of the same family, and we need to make a commitment to each other. How do we relate? 'Do not rebuke an older man harshly but exhort him as if he were your father. Treat younger men as brothers, older women as mothers, and younger women as sisters' (1 Timothy 5:1–2).

Who is to do the pastoral care of the church? Some might be tempted to answer 'the minister', but the Bible clearly says that we are to care for each other. One vicar anonymously wrote the following:

> visiting the sick, calling on everyone in the parish, keeping everyone in the congregation informed, is very difficult to do. It seems both vicar and congregation need to be re-educated as far as expectations are concerned.

This break with tradition can be a painful process, but one that must be achieved, probably at the risk of losing people from the congregation, if the church is to be healthy, strategic and growing.

In the first few weeks of leading my first church I discovered that my predecessor mowed church members' lawns, pruned their trees, did the shopping and even made breakfasts. His reputation among those members was that of a fine, servant-hearted Baptist minister. The members concerned were quick to let me know that! The expectations placed upon me by those members were huge. I then discovered that the number of folk in the church who had been served in these practical ways was limited. One minister could not meet these needs for more than a dozen or so people. This had the potential for limiting the size of the church. I managed to reject those expectations of me and accepted the responsibility of developing a wider strategy of pastoral care.

Caring for one another doesn't happen automatically, any more than other aspects of church life happen automatically. There needs to be an intentional process. There needs to be a strategy. The following steps can be part of just such a strategy.

Care for everybody

The Bible tells us that we should care for everybody, and that it is everybody's responsibility to care. Leaders set the pace, as they develop an attitude of care within the church. The principle of caring for everybody is a good place to begin a wider strategy of pastoral care.

Care for everybody, even those who don't agree with you. This is particularly pertinent for leaders. Not everybody will agree with the direction in which the church is moving, and leaders will have opponents and critics. Caring for them does not mean changing the direction of the church in order to please them. Even those who may oppose much that happens in the church are people to be cared for. Some people may be considered as what has been referred to as EGRs – 'Extra Grace Required'! We tend to think of that as a description that fits other people but of course never fits ourselves.

Care for everybody needs to overflow into the community. A strategic church is usually one that has a reputation for being a caring church. The same principles apply. Care for those who may oppose the church and are antagonistic towards it, just as much as you care for those who favour the church.

Care for those whose lifestyle may be contrary to Christian values. Show encouragement, not embarrassment. Jesus was not embarrassed by the woman caught in the act of adultery (John 8:1–11) or the woman he met at the well (John 4:1–26). Don't distance yourself from those with whom you disagree. Don't draw back. That only exacerbates the situation. Instead, show love and care. Talk *with* people, not *to* them. Emphasise becoming a disciple of Christ rather than lecturing them on the rights and wrongs of a lifestyle.

The goal is to attract people to Jesus. Jesus' strongest words of rebuke were for the religious leaders and those who should have known better. His attitude is summed up in his words, 'For God did not send his Son into the world to condemn the world, but to save the world through him' (John 3:17). Everybody you meet is a creation of God, made in his image for his purposes and someone Christ loved enough to die for. Seeing people through these lenses often changes the way we relate to them. No one we meet is a total stranger. We know at least two things about them: they were made in the image of God, and Christ died on the cross for them. In that sense, everybody we meet is 'a blessing'.

Activate a pastoral care scheme

This is where an intentional strategy can be helpful to make sure that nobody slips through the net of care. Such a scheme as this is not intended to let people off the hook of caring for one another. It is simply to ensure that care does take place. In my experience the best pastoral care schemes work through a structure of small groups where people can easily be missed if they are not there, and also where people can share their needs openly and more deeply with one another.

Small group fellowship and pastoral care, plus large group celebration, may be in fact the church of the future. This is how it was in Acts. The future could be churches large enough to attract thousands but small enough to have a personal touch. Small groups are for a number of purposes, including discipling, worship, nurturing, mission and fellowship, but also pastoral care and support. They are the key to the growth of the church, but also the key to pastoral care, particularly in the larger churches.

The amount of pastoral care that comes out of small groups can be amazing. This will be in sharp contrast to where there are no small groups or where individual members are resistant to small groups. It is harder to care for one another without this kind of structure. Sadly, some people have felt uncared for in churches, and it has been partly because they have not joined a small group. A visit by a minister or a church leader cannot replace the support of a small group where all kinds of practical help can be offered. However, where there are no small groups or where people are resistant to joining them, there still needs to be a pastoral care scheme in operation. Just because someone will not join a small group does not mean that we abdicate our responsibility to care for them as best we know how.

Remember people's names

Remembering people's names comes more easily to some than to others. If it is something that you have difficulty with, then I can only say, 'Work at it.' There are many schemes generally available that suggest ways in which you can remember people's names, but it is easier in small groups where people meet regularly.

Include the neighbours

Include praying for people beyond the congregation. One of the ways in which you can do this is to invite members of your congregation each to draw a picture of the area in which they live – the road or street. Ask them to draw a box for each house, and to include at least 20 homes. Inside each box they should list the people who live in that house and add anything that they may know about them, including the place where they may be on a spiritual journey. If your members don't know who lives around them, suggest they start inviting them in for coffee. Part of caring for people is getting to know them and remembering to pray for them. To draw the kind of picture just mentioned gives people a prayer list. It also creates an avenue of communication for hearing when people are in need. In this way a relationship has already begun to be built to enable members of your congregation to care for their neighbours.

Notify other agencies

Notify whoever needs to know. Caring for one another doesn't mean that you do everything yourself. Members of the church sometimes need to inform leaders about folk who are in need.

Sometimes specialist care is needed, and you need to know who to refer to for that specialist help. There are several of what we might call 'helping professions' that we need a link to, for example the medical, legal, social work and teaching professions. Why not issue a small leaflet called 'Where to go for help' that people in the church can be aware of, so that they know whom to turn to before a particular need arises? This is all part of working together as a team.

Generate an attitude of caring

This can be done through preaching. For example, why not preach on the 'one another's' in the New Testament – forgiving one another, loving one another, bearing one another's burdens, etc.? Like so many other attitudes in a community, the attitude of caring can be contagious.

The attitude with which we are to care for one another within the Christian community is one that admits that we ourselves need to be cared for.

> The Christian fellowship is by its very nature a covenanted group of weak, sinful and needy persons. Our awareness of our sense of need has brought us to God in Christ. Our very belonging to the church is a confession of our need for each other's help in dealing with the stresses and strains, the stumblings and fallings, the accidents and the dark difficulties that we cannot understand or accept.[1]

Honour other people

Honour other people, especially the elderly. 'Honour one another above yourselves' (Romans 12:10). There is a tendency in some churches to overlook older people both in the church and in the

---

[1] Wayne Oates, *Where to Go for Help*, Westminster Press 1957, p. 9.

community. Include them as much as possible. Care schemes within the community, such as luncheon clubs, art clubs and other activities, express care for those in the senior years of life.

Explain how your scheme works

One of the weaknesses in some churches is that a care scheme is in place but not everybody knows how it operates; consequently they do not know how to use it or call upon it. The strategy needs to be explained to newcomers, and then it needs to be repeated at regular intervals to the whole congregation. Any changes to the scheme also need to be explained.

Appoint pastoral carers

Most pastoral care schemes include appointing leaders, particularly in the larger churches, to ensure that a pastoral care scheme is working. These appointments need to be carefully made. They need to be workers who have been tried and tested in other areas, people with a real heart for pastoral care, and perhaps with some kind of training, and of course people who can be trusted with confidential information. In some instances it may be wise to take up references before making an appointment. A job description should be drawn up with a list of qualities that such an appointed person needs to have.

Revise your strategy

Whatever strategies are in place for pastoral care, don't think of them as being set in stone. The ministries are not there to serve the strategies: the strategies are there to serve the ministries. Build into the overall strategy of the church a culture of change and flexibility. That itself is part of the overall strategy.

Teach the biblical principles of care

Continually keep before the congregation the biblical principles of care. This of course is part of the Christian lifestyle, and such passages as Romans 12:9–21 and Colossians 3:12–17 spell out the kind of people we should be. If our congregations lived by the many principles found in those sections of Scripture, then our churches would indeed be beacons in the community. The brilliance of the church would shine for everyone to see.

The Bible reminds us by means of the apostle Peter's first letter that 'you are a chosen people, a royal priesthood, a holy nation, a people belonging to God, that you may declare the praises of him who called you out of darkness into his wonderful light' (1 Peter 2:9).

In many ways, this chapter might have been the first in this book. Caring for one another and caring for those who as yet do not know Jesus Christ personally is the key to everything.

11

Putting It All Together

Having read through the previous chapters you may well be asking, 'How do I put all this together? Where do I find the time?'

As already stated, there are many expectations and demands placed upon church leaders, particularly full-time pastors. Much of what you have read you will already be putting into practice. There is nothing particularly new in any of it. As said in Chapter 1, although we do not know what shape or form the church of the future will take, there are tried and tested principles based on biblical teaching that need to be implemented in every situation. Everybody is at a different point in their journey with God, and in their experience of ministry and leadership. Some of what you have read is by no means new, but it may be a matter of intentionality. The truth is that all of us know and believe far more than we are actually putting into practice. Others may be thinking, 'I would like to do all this, but where do I begin?' The answer that was given to me some years ago is simple: learn to walk before you run, or even fly. And then move one step at a time.

One of the big issues raised is that of time. The reality is that we have to learn to manage our time. It is so easy to say 'I haven't got time', and yet we all have the same amount; therefore it is a question of how we use it. Some people are very disciplined in their use of time, while others are very casual about it and let things just flow over them. The truth is that you either manage your time or your time controls you. So how do we balance all that we have got to do in our ministry? The Bible says, 'Be very careful, then, how you live – not as unwise but as wise, making the most of every opportunity' (Ephesians 5:15–16). 'Be very careful' means we need to look carefully at how we use our time. There are very many time management courses available, but most of them come down to three things:

1. Review your use of time. Carefully evaluate your diary. Learn how you use your time. Make a time log. If you have not done this before, find out how you spent your time over the last week, or even month. Check where your time goes. Making a record of how you use your time will help you to make better use of it.

2. Secondly, make the most of every opportunity. Without being legalistic, look at time in blocks. See how you might use a one-hour block or a fifteen-minute block, or even a five-minute block. Be alert to the possibilities of what you can do in a five-minute block of time. Procrastination is probably our biggest enemy. We are tempted to say, 'I've only got five or ten minutes left, so I'll put that off until tomorrow.'

Find out not only how you spend your time but also how you may waste it. Try to eliminate those occasions. Please don't misunderstand me: I do not mean that we should live such a highly disciplined life that we become legalistic, always looking at our watches. But I do believe that as Christians we are to make the best use of our time, as the Bible frequently reminds us, for we only have one life to live and we want to live it for the glory of God. We all need times of recreation, refreshment and rest. Don't see those occasions as wasting time. It is good to set aside a whole day or a whole week, or even more, when we do not have to be so conscious of time but we are using that day, that week or that month for rest and refreshment. That principle is clearly established in Scripture:

> By the seventh day God had finished the work he had been doing; so on the seventh day he rested from all his work. And God blessed the seventh day and made it holy, because on it he rested from all the work of creating that he had done. (Genesis 2:2–3)

Those occasions when we are not conscious of time are wonderful, but they need to be planned into our schedule, just as much as other activities in life, otherwise they will not happen. There are very many leaders who are tired and weary, not because they have no time, but because they are not managing their time constructively.

3. Thirdly, prioritise what is important. For Christians, it simply comes down to trying to do what God wants us to do: in other words, doing God's will and fulfilling his purposes as best we know how.

So how do we go about building a strategic church? Well, of course it is God who builds his church, and he wants it to be strategic. We simply want to be in on what he wants to do in our area.

First of all, someone must take the lead. Secondly, build the team. Thirdly, create relational structures. Then change something that, if you are the main preacher, is probably the easiest to change, and that is your preaching, so that it becomes more relevant and has more emphasis on application. Train and equip others. Think exponentially. Have a generous spirit. Get involved with the community. And, most important, have a caring heart.

Having a strategy for your church has nothing to do with its size; nothing to do with its denomination; nothing to do with its style of worship; but it has everything to do with commitment to the Great Commission.

You may have expected this book to give you a number of examples of strategic churches. However, that can be dangerous, as leaders are tempted to try to imitate them. I do not want to open up that temptation to readers, and there are very many other books that describe models of church. My hope is that leaders, with God's help, will implement the principles identified and develop them into a unique strategic church. I know that to do this some leaders and congregations may have to learn new skills. I would encourage you to do the work. Spiritual growth and church health are not automatic processes. They are the result of praying and planning and practical application. Strategic churches are those with a high resolve that they will do whatever it takes to present Christ to this generation, 'using today's technology and language to present the transforming message of Christ with impeccable clarity'.[1]

Post-Christendom has created a desire for change and for something new and different. Some recent headlines from Christian newspapers are testimony to this:

○ 'The Church needs a new orientation'
○ 'Clear strategies are required'
○ 'New churches for a new age'
○ 'Time to re-shape the church'

Time and again we read articles and hear seminars encouraging different ways of being the church.

* * * *

[1] From the webpage of Ron Sylvia (author of *Starting High Definition Churches*).

- ○ 'We need to be churches without walls.'
- ○ 'We have to take the good news out into the world.'
- ○ 'We need to step out into the community instead of expecting the community to come to us.'
- ○ 'We must be prepared to pay the price of mission.'
- ○ 'We need to take risks.'
- ○ 'It's time for a new missionary zeal.'
- ○ 'The churches need to step out of their comfort zone.'
- ○ 'We need a new confidence in taking the good news out of the confines of the church and into the world.'
- ○ 'This is the time for social care initiatives and partnering with local authorities.'
- ○ 'It's time for radical church planting.'
- ○ 'It's time to change attitudes and buildings and practices in order to reach people for Christ.'
- ○ 'The church must be serious about mission.'

We can be overwhelmed by such headlines and encouragements and challenges. Many of the statements are true, but how do we respond? I believe we should gather as much information as possible. Read books on church health and growth. Attend those conferences that appear to offer help. However, having gathered so much information, what do you do with it? I believe the best way to use all of the accumulated information, expertise and experience is to root it firmly in the biblical principles of being church. In many ways we have made church too complicated. I am amazed sometimes at just how complex some churches are. The basic unit of church is two or three people meeting regularly to help one another to live the life of authentic disciples. That is a wholesome strategy.

We must not, however, lose sight of the fact that God wants his church to grow. There is a sense of great celebration in the story that unfolds in the Acts of the Apostles. The statistics that are mentioned are mentioned for a reason and are important. We should count people, because people matter. The parable of the one lost sheep should occupy our attention. It shows that the shepherd counted, because he knew when one was missing. It shows too that when we are together as Christians in whatever number, whether it is a handful or many thousands, we should be concerned about the one lost sheep that is still outside the fold. All the time there is one person in your community who does not know Jesus Christ, you should be reaching out to them.

We are involved in kingdom work. We are available for God to use. In the parable of the growing seed, Jesus said,

> This is what the kingdom of God is like. A man scatters seed on the ground. Night and day, whether he sleeps or gets up, the seed sprouts and grows, though he does not know how. All by itself the soil produces corn – first the stalk, then the ear, then the full grain in the ear. As soon as the grain is ripe, he puts the sickle to it, because the harvest has come. (Mark 4:26–29)

Notice the connection. As Christian Schwarz (a Lutheran and Head of the Institute for Church Development in Germany) points out in his book *Natural Church Development*, 'this parable clearly shows what people can and should do, and what they cannot do. They should sow and harvest. What they cannot do is this: they cannot bring forth the fruit. I understand this principle to be the very essence of church growth. Some do it deliberately, others by instinct. It doesn't really matter. Ultimately, what counts is applying this principle.'[2]

Finally, having resisted the temptation to give examples of models of strategic church, here are some typical practical expressions of strategic churches.

Generally speaking, strategic churches are those that are

---

[2] Christian A. Schwarz., *Natural Church Development*, ChurchSmart Resources 1996, p. 12.

committed to reaching people in the multiplicity of life's situations. They have a well-rounded ministry of service to the community. This ministry includes spiritual life development, evangelism and social needs. The challenge is put before the congregation to meet the total needs of the total community. Some of these churches have proved that you do not need elaborate buildings and structures to create a dynamic ministry. These are churches where people come every weekend to worship and then immerse themselves into the community through the life of their church. The tendency is to think that we must have many gifted people to fulfil this type of ministry, when all it really takes is vision and people, a people committed to serve Jesus Christ on a genuine biblical basis.

Strategic churches are those that attempt to uncover the needs of the community. Some of these churches assume the challenge of visiting everybody in the community, knocking on the doors of thousands of homes. One pastor undertook to do this himself. He averaged ten calls a day, excluding Sunday. It was a massive task, but he undertook it and accomplished it, visiting every home in his local community. He asked those he called on the question, 'What would you like the church to do for you?' If he got a sensible answer that expressed a genuine need, he would reply either 'We are able to do that now' or 'We do not yet have the resources to meet that need, but as soon as we are able to meet that need we will be back and serve you as best we can.' In this way he learned of the genuine needs of the community.

On one of his visits a woman said, 'I'm Jewish.' She was about to slam the door, but the pastor stopped her and said, 'I'm going to preach on Abraham this coming Sunday', to which the lady replied, 'Who?' 'Abraham,' he said. She shot back, 'Who in the world is Abraham?' The pastor explained that he was the father of the Jewish people. The woman, somewhat surprised, asked, 'Where did you find that out?' The pastor replied, 'In the Bible, in the Old Testament.' The lady replied, 'Well, I've heard something about the Bible. I might be there.' And then she did slam the door. The very next Sunday the lady turned up at church. And here is the point: the pastor later confessed, 'That changed my style of preaching.' He learned to get on the wavelength of a very diverse community.

In many communities it would be difficult to visit door to door. There are other ways of discovering community needs, but it must be done with a systematic, sympathetic approach. Vague methods will not accomplish the task. Strategic churches do it correctly. If you were to take ten of the most strategic churches in the country (they could be different sizes, not necessarily large), you would probably find that although each one has a different approach to its ministry, each has found the key to reaching the community with its needs for Christ. Some churches have accomplished this through small groups scattered throughout the community; others have done it through seeker services. Some have done it through meeting social needs in the community; others have done it through filling in gaps in community life by providing such things as a sports ministry, an Internet café, or places where people can meet together and share common interests. A new awareness of where people are in their lives, home, family and work becomes absolutely vital. The innovative strategic church can step into such situations and develop an effective ministry.

Let Jim Cymbala of Brooklyn Tabernacle in New York, a very strategic church, have the final word:

> Let us never accept the excuse that God cannot work in *our* situation
> . . . that our particular people are too rich, or too poor . . . too inner-
> city or too suburban . . . too traditional or too avant-garde. This kind
> of thinking is never found in the Word of God. No matter what ethnic
> origin or geography characterizes the local church, we *can* see God do

things just as he did in the book of Acts, since he has *never* changed. The only changing that can occur is within us. Let us purpose in our hearts to change in his direction and see him do incredible things to the praise of the glory of his grace.[3]

---

[3] Jim Cymbala, *Fresh Wind, Fresh Fire*, Zondervan 1997, p. 184.

Appendix 1

How whole-life is your church?

1. Our church is trying as a community to picture and pray for the people of the church in their daily activities. Yes ☐ No ☐
2. Our church is a safe place to have questions and doubts, and values them as an opportunity to learn and grow in faith. Yes ☐ No ☐
3. Our church encourages us to take our local, national and global citizenship seriously and to engage in issues of justice and community action. Yes ☐ No ☐
4. Our church creates opportunities to tell and hear each other's stories. Yes ☐ No ☐
5. Our church actively tries to help every member understand the basic teachings and skills of the Christian life. Yes ☐ No ☐
6. Our church encourages us to find out the key pressure points for a small number of people and to pray for them. Yes ☐ No ☐
7. Our church encourages us to develop hospitality in ways that allow not-yet-believers to enjoy our Christian friends. Yes ☐ No ☐
8. Our church is a place where creativity can flourish. Yes ☐ No ☐
9. Our church recognises the main questions that not-yet-Christians have about our faith and helps us learn how to handle them. Yes ☐ No ☐

10. Our church actively supports people who are trying to bring kingdom values into their sphere of influence, such as the arts, business, politics, justice and education. Yes ☐ No ☐

11. Our church helps us learn how to use our contemporary culture – things such as films, work experiences, news – to learn more about what it means to follow Jesus. Yes ☐ No ☐

12. Our church encourages us to reflect on what we are learning at the moment. Yes ☐ No ☐

13. Our church is actively trying to help us gain practical wisdom for some of life's major challenges in our home lives, such as parenting, singleness, marriage, sickness and death. Yes ☐ No ☐

14. Our church commissions and prays for people's new jobs and responsibilities outside the church as well as inside. Yes ☐ No ☐

15. Our church provokes us to pray regularly for a not-yet-believer in the life of one of our Christian friends. Yes ☐ No ☐

16. Our church helps us deepen our understanding of the 'human Jesus' in his context, so we can learn to be like him in ours. Yes ☐ No ☐

17. Our corporate prayer diary or prayer meetings show a good balance between the needs of the local church 'scattered', the church 'gathered', and the national and global issues we face, such as consumerism and poverty. Yes ☐ No ☐

18. The leaders in our church model ways of helping individuals mature in faith and life. Yes ☐ No ☐

19. Our church reflects on why the gospel is good news for us at work, at home, in the community, in society – today, as well as for our future. Yes ☐ No ☐

20. Our church helps us handle the tensions of suffering as well as joy, of failure as well as success. Yes ☐ No ☐

© *Let My People Grow*, LICC, 2005

Appendix 2

Preaching for life change

This is a course taught by Rick Warren, Senior Pastor of Saddleback Community Church, and author of *The Purpose Driven Church* and *The Purpose Driven Life*. It's available from Purpose Driven UK.

The sessions covered are:

The purpose of preaching

Preaching must be in harmony with God's overall purpose for people's lives to develop Christ-like convictions, character and conduct. Learn how to become a purpose driven communicator through this insightful and eye-opening session. Discover God's purpose for those whom he has called to preach the life-changing message of Jesus Christ.

How to C.R.A.F.T. a message

Collect and categorise

Success is the management of good ideas. Everybody has good ideas – the issue is what you do with them. Preachers must be in the habit of gathering materials and ideas for messages. Learn four ways to collect material, including how to find relevant Bible study helps, and how to create a simple system for collecting, filing, preserving and retrieving information.

Research and reflect

Researching means you study with your mind: that's the technical part of the sermon. Reflection means you listen with your heart: that's the devotional part of the sermon. Through this seminar, discover resources to help you with your exegesis, and then learn six ways to meditate upon the text.

Apply and arrange

Learn three ways to provide Scripture application so that you can challenge the congregation and individuals through your messages, and then hear nine ideas on outlining a message for maximum impact.

Fashion and flavour

How do you choose the right words? Join Rick as he explains the key to becoming a word-smith, one who uses specific words to bridge the gap between truth and application. Learn about three 'Flavour Enhancers', as well as how to season your messages with illustrations, quotations, humour, video clips, testimonies, drama and interviews.

Trim and Tie Together

There's an art to trimming content to make your messages more effective. Learn how to cut content and then how to tie the introduction, conclusion and transitions together to form the purpose of your message. You'll also learn new ways to call your congregation to commitment and how to give a life-changing invitation.

Appendix 3

S.H.A.P.E. is about finding your unique purpose in life. It was devised several years ago by Rick Warren, Senior Pastor of Saddleback Community Church in California, to help people discover how God's five purposes can be fulfilled in their lives. He believed that God didn't design ministry for just the few with theology degrees but designed every believer to play a unique role in the local church.

Over the years the concept has been developed, and S.H.A.P.E. is now available as a training tool with workshop material enabling people to discover their:

Spiritual gifts
Heart
Abilities
Personality
Experiences

This ensemble of passions, talents, experiences, temperament and other components work together to make you who you are.

As well as the S.H.A.P.E. workshop materials, a new book has been written by Erik Rees, one of the pastors at Saddleback, to help everyone discover God's unique purpose in life based on the way God has *shaped* them.

By using the S.H.A.P.E. materials you can discover how to mobilise your church for 'every member ministry', as each member discovers their own unique way of ministering to others in need.

Both materials and book are available from Purpose Driven UK.

Appendix 4

The purpose driven covenant

Today I am stepping across the line. I'm tired of waffling, and I'm finished with wavering, I've made my choice, the verdict is in and my decision is irrevocable. I'm going God's way. There's no turning back now!

I will live the rest of my life serving God's purposes with God's people on God's planet for God's glory. I will use my life to celebrate his presence, cultivate his character, participate in his family, demonstrate his love and communicate his word.

Since my past has been forgiven, and I have a purpose for living, and a home awaiting in heaven, I refuse to waste any more time or energy on shallow living, petty thinking, trivial talking, thoughtless doing, useless regretting, hurtful resenting or faithless worrying. Instead I will magnify God, grow to maturity, serve in ministry and fulfil my mission in the membership of his family.

Because this life is preparation for the next, I will value worship over wealth, 'we' over 'me', character over comfort, service over status, and people over possessions, position and pleasures. I know what matters most, and I'll give it all I've got. I'll do the best I can with what I have for Jesus Christ today.

I won't be captivated by culture, manipulated by critics, motivated by praise, frustrated by problems, debilitated by temptation or intimidated by the devil. I'll keep running my race with my eyes on the goal, not the sidelines or those running by me. When times get tough, and I get tired, I won't back up, back off, back down, back out or backslide. I'll just keep moving forward by God's grace. I'm Spirit-led, purpose-driven and mission-focused, so I cannot be bought, I will not be compromised, and I shall not quit until I finish the race.

I'm a trophy of God's amazing grace, so I will be gracious to everyone, grateful for every day and generous with everything that God entrusts to me.

To my Lord and Saviour Jesus Christ, I say: *However, whenever, wherever, and whatever* you ask me to do, my answer in advance is yes! Wherever you lead and whatever the cost, I'm ready. Anytime, anywhere, anyway. *Whatever it takes, Lord; whatever it takes!* I want to be used by you in such a way that on that final day I'll hear you say, 'Well done, thou good and faithful one. Come on in and let the eternal party begin!'

Appendix 5

Faithworks is a movement of thousands of individuals, churches and organisations motivated by their Christian faith to serve the needs of their local communities and positively influence society as a whole. Steve Chalke inspired the idea of a Faithworks Movement and laid the foundations for its launch as a campaign in February 2001, through its founding partner, the Oasis Trust. The Revd Malcolm Duncan is the leader of Faithworks, with responsibility for inspiring, leading and developing the movement globally.

The following article by Malcolm Duncan is reproduced with his permission:

'Too many cooks spoil the broth!' That's the cry of many church leaders and Christians when it comes to partnership and working with others. The thought of having to go to meetings and do everything by committee drives overworked and underpaid Christians crazy a lot of the time. Yet there are also many Christian leaders who cry 'Many hands make light work!' They have discovered a depth of fellowship, achievement and purpose in working with others that has transformed the way they think about working with other people. The two seem to be completely contradictory – but which does the Bible encourage?

Theology of partnership

Well, the straightforward answer is partnership! Without it, Adam and Eve ran into a great deal of trouble! The twelve tribes of Israel worked best when they worked together. The commands for the building of the Temple and its function, the transporting of the tabernacle and the construction of the ark – all of these demanded detailed and demanding partnership. Add to these examples the fact that Jesus commissioned disciples to work in teams, called twelve people to be the pillars of his church and that the apostle Paul always worked in teams, and you have pretty strong biblical support for partnership. The church is built on body ministry – and scriptures like Ephesians 4, 1 Corinthians 12, Romans 12 and Peter's letters all make it really clear that working together is vital to the success of the church. And of course, God himself is a partnership of three personalities working in perfect harmony. Perhaps the most poignant example of scriptural encouragement to partnership is the deeply emotional and moving prayer of Jesus himself in John 17 – that the world might know that we are one. The evidence is pretty overwhelming theologically! There are lots of other, more pragmatic reasons for working in partnership, though.

Opportunities and benefits

When churches work together they share resources, avoid duplication and give one another mutual support. The lonely youth worker suddenly finds another lonely youth worker, and the two support and encourage one another! You also discover a strengthened vision when working with others – after all, two sets of eyes can see the same thing very differently – and one complements the other. You also increase the chances of meeting the right people at the right time when you work with others, because you open up more contacts from two address books than you do from one. The very fact that one church has a certain tradition and set of contacts while another moves in different spheres of influence is a good reason for working together.

Not only that, but when you work with other churches, you can suddenly claim to represent much more of your community, and your voice is strengthened by working with others. One person can shout, but 100 people can roar! This kind of joint working leads to strengthened credibility and a much more reliable reputation. Would you rather be known as someone who people can work with or someone who can't work with others? How do you think Jesus would be described today?

Perhaps the most obvious benefit of partnership is the fact that you can each benefit from one another. Mistakes don't have to be repeated, and good lessons are always worth learning. Partnership gives you an opportunity to avoid the pitfalls others have fallen into and take the right decision at the right time.

Obstacles

Despite the theological and pragmatic benefits of partnership, it would be naïve to suggest that there are not a number of obstacles to working together. The biggest obstacle is pride. We can fool ourselves into thinking that we are the only ones who know the answers, that God can use our church only, or that our theology is tighter and better than anyone else's. Of course, none of these are true, but ego is a powerful thing! We can dress it up as much as we like, but if we think that we always know best, then there is a problem deep within our hearts or our church that we need to address.

It can also be really hard to build trust with people that we have been distanced from for years. You don't overcome that kind of distance with one call and a coffee – but you can at least make a start. Sometimes initial contact with others can be a challenge, but we shouldn't let that initial difficulty put us off. The challenges of committees, teams and bureaucracy can also get in the way of partnering – but only if we let them.

The biggest obstacle to partnering is the fear that we will have a clash of culture or identity. But we need to learn that we do not need to agree with everything someone does to partner with them. I don't need to weaken my Christian identity to work with non-Christian organisations. Instead, I need to be sure of my identity and certain about when I can partner and when I cannot. Sometimes you have to make it really clear what you can do and what you cannot do. There are things we can support and things we cannot support as Christians. But perhaps if we discover and live out our clear Christian faith and identity, the only exclusion that will take place is when others decide they cannot accept who we are or what we stand for. That is a challenge that many of us need to learn to understand and live out.

You do not need to compromise to partner, but you do need to be open to learning, growing and changing through the input of others. Christians face discrimination because of our distinctives, but we should be the champions of distinctive faith and partnership meeting the diverse needs of our communities. Partnership challenges us to think through who we are, what we really believe, and what is essential and what is not. We need to learn different language and customs and activities. But that is exactly what we ask people to do every time we invite new people to come to our church services!

Quick guide to partnership

Here is a quick guide to help you work out how you can partner effectively. It is by no means exhaustive, but it will start your thinking – all the best!

1. Work out who you are and what you have to offer

Churches have vision, experience, understanding of the community, commitment to long-term solutions, buildings and strong local knowledge. You need to work out what this means for you, your congregation and the community where God has placed you. Why has God placed you there? Who are the other people at work in your community? Ask yourself which of those groups you can work with and how you can help them. What are the non-negotiables for you as a church? Be careful not to enshrine your preferences here – what are the essential and the non-essential things for you and your faith? Let them shape whom you work with.

You can bring a holistic approach to your community. You can be more relational than some other groups. You can offer more in-depth and focused support to individuals. You can reach people that others cannot – the traditionally under-represented and excluded people in your community. Also, don't forget that you can bring the hope of a fresh start, true transformation, and real purpose and hope through what you do. All of those are pretty strong and unique contributions of the church to a community or a project. David Blunkett has said this:

> Faith groups are a resource available to all areas of the country, even the most deprived, the least active and the most likely to be disengaged from the political process. This is a resource that every government regeneration programme cannot match.

2. Focus on your strengths and areas of common interest

Partner on the issues you feel strongly about! Decide what resources you have, then target them in a thought-through and effective way. A small church cannot partner in hundreds of projects, but your contribution could make a real difference in one. So work out what you are really passionate about in your community and then make every effort to get involved in something that will make a difference in that area.

3. Signpost

One of the key elements of partnership is recognising that you do not have to do everything yourself! Learn the art of referring people to others in your area. You may not be able to help a young teenage mum with a flat and food and clothes. But by partnering with others in your town, you can become part of a wide network of people who have a broad spread of resources. If you aren't at the table, you don't share in the feast.

4. Find mutual benefit

Partnership should be beneficial to you and to others – so find the common ground and the common benefit. But be careful! Always be ready to give yourself away. Partner because it is right, not just because it is good for you. Every now and then God challenges us to give away the best of ourselves in partnership – after all, that is what he did.

Where to from here?

Well, the whistle-stop tour of partnership has ended. Just one last encouragement – speak the right language! Learn to articulate hope in words that non-Christians understand. We talk about the 'poor', the government talks about the 'excluded'. We talk about having a heart for our communities, the government talks about community cohesion. We talk about a prophetic role, the government talks about empowering others. We talk about loving our neighbour, and the government talks about mutual support and social capital. We talk about helping people fulfil their potential in Christ, the government talks about supporting people!

Whatever you do as you think about partnering, in your head and in your heart, do it for Jesus.

Bibliography

Paul Beasley-Murray, *Transform Your Church*, IVP 2005.

Neil Cole, *Organic Church*, Leadership Network 2005.

Jim Cymbala, *Fresh Wind: Fresh Fire*, Zondervan 1997.

Lewis A. Drummond, *Eight Keys to Spiritual Revival*, Bethany House Publishers 1994.

Lewis A. Drummond, *Ripe for Harvest*, Broadman Press 2001.

Lewis A. Drummond, *The Word of the Cross*, Broadman Press, 1992.

Eddie Gibbs and Ian Coffey, *Church Next*, IVP 2001.

Bill and Lynne Hybels, *Rediscovering Church*, Zondervan 1995.

Larry Michael, *Spurgeon on Leadership*, Kregel, 2003.

Sally Morgenthaler, *Worship Evangelism*, Zondervan 1995.

Harold Myra and Shelley Marshall, *The Leadership Secrets of Billy Graham*, Zondervan 2005.

Neil Pugmire, *100 Ways to Get Your Church Noticed*, Kingsway Publications 2006.

Thom Rainer, *The Book of Church Growth*, Broadman, 1993.

Christian A. Schwarz, *Natural Church Development*, ChurchSmart Resources 1996.

Dan Southerland, *Transitioning*, Zondervan 2000.

Rick Warren, *The Purpose Driven Church*, Zondervan 1995.

Rick Warren, *The Purpose Driven Life*, Zondervan 2002.

Further Reading

Leith Anderson, *A Church for the 21st Century*, Bethany House Publishers 1992.

Mike Breen and Walt Kallestad, *The Passionate Church*, Cook Communications Ministries 2005.

C. B. Hogue, *I Want My Church to Grow*, Broadman Press 1977.

Philip Jenkins, *The Next Christendom*, Oxford University Press 2002.

Michael Moynagh, *Changing World, Changing Church*, Monarch 2001.

Eric Rees, *S.H.A.P.E.*, Zondervan 2006.

James Emery White, *Re-thinking the Church*, Baker Books 1997.

Resources

www.strategicchurch.co.uk

Keep up to date with Strategic Church Conferences. This site will provide follow-up resource material and links to other 'strategic' sites. It will be updated with ideas, worthwhile quotes and articles, plus tools to help you build a strategic church. From time to time there will also be relevant book reviews.

* * *

Other useful sites include:

Christian Research – **www.christian-research.org.uk**

Evangelical Alliance – **www.eauk.org**

Faithworks – **www.faithworks.info**

Imagine Project set up by the London Institute of Contemporary Christianity – **www.licc.org.uk**

Mind the Gap – **www.agape.org.uk** *Mind the Gap* is a set of DVD-based workshops to help church leaders and their congregations think through their approach to evangelism among the un-churched. It's not a personal evangelism course, nor a blueprint on how to do it. Rather, it's lots of good, tried and tested ideas on how to build in good practice and some creativity, while gaining the enthusiastic involvement of church members.

Purpose Driven for 40 Days of Purpose and 40 Days of Community – **www.purposedrivenuk.com**

Simply Strategic, a ministry of Granger Community Church, Indiana. Their blogs and podcast are:

○ Tonymorganlive.com
○ Leadingsmart.com
○ Simplystrategicshow.blogspot.com

Tony Morgan, one of the pastors at Granger Community Church (GCCwired.com), recently listed '10 Questions Growing Churches Should Ask' on his website:

1. Is your ministry strategy creating buzz in your community?
2. Do volunteers own the ministry of the church?
3. Do you exceed the expectations of your first-time guests?
4. Are you attracting the very best talent to your team?
5. Are people having fun?
6. Does your team know, embrace and champion the church's established vision and values?
7. Do people accept change as normal?
8. Are you addressing the real issues of real lives?
9. Are you as committed to developing effective systems as you are to innovation?
10. Have you built a church of leaders?

For further resources look on their website: **www.wiredchurches.com**

50 Ways to Help Your Church Grow

by David Beer

There's a mountain of books on the mission of the church. There are books that diagnose the spiritual state of the nation. There are books on leadership styles, how to initiate change and how to manage it. There are conferences to motivate you, Bible weeks to renew your vision.

But it's Monday morning and you have people to visit and meetings to prepare. And there's a building to worry about, and junk mail to junk.

How do you tread the path between vision and reality? How do you get all that unrealised potential out of the pew and into the street? And how do you turn the tide from being a surviving church to a thriving church?

'This is a book filled with hope! If put into practice, I believe it could bring about a mighty spiritual awakening that could touch every city and town and bring many to Christ.'

Rick Warren, Pastor of Saddleback Church and
author of The Purpose-Driven Church

'David Beer is a natural communicator. He knows from experience that effective ministry requires a motivated team with a clear vision and a sharp spiritual focus. This book gives you the whole picture.'

Michael Talbot, Series Editor, ITV's *Sunday Morning* programme

'This book provides us with the tools to get many churches out of the rut of spiritual dryness and irrelevance and on to the road of health and growth.'

Steve Chalke, TV presenter and Baptist Minister

 Kingsway

Releasing Your Church to Grow

by David Beer

'If you are looking for a biblical, balanced, and proven example of what it means to be a purpose-driven church in a British context, the answer is in your hand. David Beer is a visionary pastor who is modelling for all of us what it means to take the Great Commandment and Great Commission seriously. I highly recommend this book. Read it. Study it. Practise it!'

Rick Warren

'Every church that David has led has grown – and grown dramatically. It's this combination of understanding and delivery that makes this book different.'

Steve Chalke

'From purpose to preparation, from structure to small groups, David covers the basics. This book takes the complicated challenge of getting a church healthy and focused, and breaks it down into simple bite-size pieces. The best thing about this book is that it is do-able by the average pastor.'

From the foreword by Dan Southerland
Director of Church Transitions Inc.